BUSINESS ETHICS IN UNCERTAIN TIMES

Business Ethics in Uncertain Times

Marian Burk Wood, M.B.A.

Upper Saddle River, New Jersey 07458

Acquisitions editor: David Parker
Assistant editor: Ashley Keim
Production editor: Carol Zaino
Manufacturer: Courier (Bookmart Press, Inc.)

ISBN 0-13-141422-4

10 9 8 7 6 5 4 3 2

TABLE OF CONTENTS

PREFACE

Inflated earnings. Insider trading. Conflicts of interest. These are only three of the difficult ethical issues making news these days. As former executives are being arrested (or are pleading guilty) on charges ranging from conspiring to defraud shareholders to misusing corporate funds, federal regulators and state attorneys general continue to scrutinize the questionable actions of other managers and accountants. Yet, despite the few who have exercised poor judgment and made unethical decisions, the vast majority of businesspeople are careful to respect the prevailing legal and ethical guidelines of our society.

Business Ethics In Uncertain Times, designed as a supplement to Prentice Hall business and management textbooks, provides an in-depth analysis of today's most vital ethical challenges. The supplement also includes six insightful news articles dissecting the ethical problems of Enron, Arthur Andersen, and WorldCom. Exercises at the end of every chapter reinforce important points and challenge students to consider how managers can and should respond to the different ethical issues they face on the job. A listing of ethics resources online describes Web sites where students can find corporate codes of conduct and a wealth of other ethics-related information.

Organization of this Supplement

Chapter 1 introduces the basics of contemporary business ethics by defining business ethics, examining five approaches to resolving ethical issues, and discussing the goals and conflicts that organizations face in managing stakeholder relations.

Chapter 2 presents a number of key issues in business ethics, including management responsibility, corporate governance, accounting practices, and approaches to instilling and supporting ethical decisions and behavior throughout the organization. A listing of online ethics sources appears at the end of this chapter.

Chapter 3 looks more closely at Enron's ethical challenges, starting with a brief overview of the company's situation and continuing with an article reprinted from *Insight* and an article reprinted from the *New York Times*.

Chapter 4 examines Arthur Andersen's ethical challenges, starting with an introduction to the accounting firm's situation and continuing with two perceptive articles reprinted from the *New York Times*.

Chapter 5 digs deeper into the ethical challenges faced by WorldCom, starting with an overview of the company's situation and continuing with an article reprinted from the *Wall Street Journal* and an article reprinted from the *New York Times*.

About the Author

Marian Burk Wood has held vice-presidential level positions in corporate and non-profit marketing with Citibank, Chase Manhattan Bank, and the National Retail Federation, as well as management positions with national retail chains. She is the author of *The Marketing Plan: A Handbook* and has co-authored college textbooks on principles of marketing (with Dr. Bill Nickels of University of Maryland), principles of management (with Courtland Bovée of Grossmont College), and principles of advertising (with Courtland Bovée of Grossmont College). Wood has also developed chapters, cases, exercises, features, and print and electronic supplements for numerous college texts in business-related disciplines. She holds an M.B.A. in marketing from Long Island University and a B.A. from the City University of New York.

With sincere thanks to the fabulous Prentice Hall team: Editor-in-Chief Jeff Shelstad; Acquisitions Editor David Parker; Assistant Editor Ashley Keim; Editorial Assistant Melissa Yu; and Permissions Coordinator Suzanne Grappi.

Marian Burk Wood
MarianBWW@netscape.net

CONTACT YOUR LOCAL PRENTICE HALL REPRESENTATIVE TO PACKAGE THIS SUPPLEMENT WITH ANY PRENTICE HALL TEXTBOOK.

RECOMMENDED TEXTS:

Introduction to Business:
Griffin/Ebert, Business
Ebert/Griffin, Business Essentials
Bovee/Thill, Business In Action
Mescon/Bovee/Thill, Business Today

Principles of Management:
Certo, Modern Management
Robbins/Coulter, Management
Robbins, Managing Today
Robbins/DeCenzo, Fundamentals of Management
Dessler, Management
Dessler, Framework for Management
Black/Porter, Management

Organizational Behavior:
Robbins, Organizational Behavior
Robbins, Essentials of Organizational Behavior
Gordon, Organizational Behavior
Greenberg/Baron, Behavior in Organizations
Greenberg, Managing Behavior in Organizations
George/Jones, Organizational Behavior

INSTRUCTOR'S TEACHING NOTES ARE AVAILABLE ON THE FACULTY SIDE OF EACH TEXT'S WEB SITE LISTED ABOVE.

Chapter 1: Introduction to Contemporary Business Ethics

OVERVIEW OF BUSINESS ETHICS

Business ethics are headline news from Texas to Tokyo. Ethical challenges in the business world are hardly new: Upton Sinclair exposed unsavory meatpacking practices in his 1906 book, *The Jungle,* leading to sweeping new U.S. regulations for pure food. However, the unprecedented scope of recent scandals has put business ethics back in the public eye all over the world. Facing the uncertainty of global economic pressures, more intense competition, closer Wall Street scrutiny, volatile markets, and wavering public confidence, some managers have made questionable decisions about ethical issues.[1]

Consider these examples of three U.S. businesses that made headlines for the way they handled ethical decisions:

- **Enron.** Once a market-leading energy company, Enron used dubious accounting practices to enhance revenues and mask liabilities. Key executives also had conflicts of interest; some were paid huge bonuses and cashed out stock holdings even as they urged employees to buy more or retain their shares of company stock while the share price plunged. The company's bankruptcy swept away much of the value of Enron employees' 401(k) retirement holdings and put thousands out of work.[2] See Chapter 3 for more about Enron's situation.

- **Arthur Andersen.** Andersen, the public accounting firm that audited Enron's financial reports, was convicted for obstructing justice during a Securities and Exchange Commission (SEC) investigation of Enron's complex financial dealings. By the time the verdict was announced, Andersen had lost hundreds of clients and thousands of employees and soon ceased auditing operations altogether. Previously Andersen paid millions of dollars in penalties for faulty audits at Waste Management and was the auditor for Sunbeam, Global Crossing, and WorldCom—which all declared bankruptcy.[3] See Chapter 4 for more about Andersen's situation.

- **WorldCom.** One of the largest U.S. telecommunications companies, WorldCom admitted it had improperly spread more than $7 billion in expenses over an extended period to make its earnings look better. Its stock price plummeted as investors jumped ship and the company finally filed for bankruptcy (the largest filing in U.S. history at that point), laying off 17,000 workers.[4] WorldCom's former chief financial officer and former controller were later arrested on charges of securities fraud. See Chapter 5 for more about the WorldCom situation.

Other major U.S. firms have been publicly criticized for ethical lapses ranging from failing to disclose huge loans to top management and controversial use of corporate funds (Adelphia) to arranging complicated transactions that make earnings look better without completely disclosing information about the practice to investors (Global Crossing).[5]

Scandals over business ethics also have erupted outside the United States. Consider the ethically questionable decisions and activities of these Japanese firms:[6]

- **Snow Brand.** The largest dairy producer in Japan, Snow Brand cut corners by recycling outdated milk and neglecting to properly clean pipes in its facilities. As a result, about 15,000 customers fell ill from its tainted milk products. Snow Brand's stock price plunged following the revelations, and its future survival is uncertain.

- **Kyowa Perfumery.** This additives manufacturer continued to sell flavorings to Kentucky Fried Chicken and other food firms in Japan even though the additives had been banned for 30 years. Once the practice came to light, food products containing the forbidden additives were recalled.

- **Universal Studios Japan.** The popular theme park disclosed that it had sold outdated salami and other old food products—some nine months past the original "sell by" date—by changing the labels. Park management also failed to notify health officials about unhealthy water in one drinking fountain; the park was later forced to close all fountains due to unacceptably high bacteria levels in the water.

The above examples describe a wide range of suspect business decisions and activities. In some cases, managers or employees took steps that were clearly illegal, such as selling food additives that had been outlawed years earlier. In other cases, managers made decisions that were not clearly illegal but could not be considered completely honest, either. What, then, is the connection between ethics and business?

Defining Business Ethics

Business ethics applies a group's standards of right and wrong to the decisions and actions of business organizations, managers, and employees. Ethical rules and standards are shaped by the society (or societies) in which the organizations and its workforce operate. In addition, managers and employees are individually guided by their own morality and their personal sense of right and wrong.[7] *Ethical management* means "acting ethically as a manager by doing the right thing."[8] This definition implies taking actions that go beyond what the law requires or allows.

Managers sometimes face *ethical dilemmas,* situations in which they must decide between two courses of action that may be equally valid.[9] No decision in such situations is definitely right or wrong. To resolve such dilemmas, the decision-maker may first weigh the potential consequences—positive, negative, or neutral—of the two actions. Who might be helped or hurt by each course of action, and what kinds of short-term and long-term consequences might each course of action entail?[10] Another approach is to examine the ethical nature of the actions themselves. Does either action violate any ethical rules or exploit the vulnerability of a particular person or group? Although such choices are difficult because they are not clear-cut, business decision-makers rely on their own ethical standards as well as those of their employers and society at large when evaluating the different courses of action and their consequences.

Among the recent business scandals dealing with financial disclosures, some fall into the category of ethical dilemmas. When a public corporation is not required to report certain complex transactions, is it deceiving its shareholders by failing to fully explain these dealings? Should executives voluntarily disclose such financial transactions if they fear that the share price may plunge, hurting shareholders and threatening the jobs of hundreds or thousands of employees?

In contrast, *ethical lapses* occur when people make decisions or take actions that clearly violate prevailing ethical or legal standards. The company managers who decided to continue selling banned additives violated the law as well as their society's moral rules. Another example of an ethical lapse: financial executives who misreport company expenses in violation of federal laws and generally accepted accounting principles (abbreviated as GAAP).

Putting Ethical Challenges into Perspective

Managers face ethical challenges in almost every aspect of an organization's operations, not just financial dealings. Marketing managers, for example, face decisions such as whether and how to advertise products like pain remedies that help relieve suffering but may be harmful if used for long periods. Sales managers face decisions about selling expensive products that may severely strain a buyer's budget. Manufacturing managers face decisions about operating factories that employ hundreds of people but generate emissions that may hurt the environment. Technology managers face decisions about gathering, analyzing, and exchanging customer and employee data in ways that may violate personal privacy.

Despite the many challenges they face, the vast majority of companies, managers, and employees respect legal and moral guidelines as they make decisions every working day. From a practical standpoint, ethical decisions make good business sense. Customers, employees, and suppliers are more attracted to firms that earn a reputation for high ethical standards. Conversely, companies that make headlines for poor ethical judgment often lose customers and employees and may even lose the support of their communities. Clearly, it is in a company's best interest to make decisions that are seen as both ethical and legal. In fact, 83 percent of employees in a recent survey said they would tell management about major frauds by coworkers—a higher proportion than in the past. "The impact that some of the recent corporate failures have had on people's lives, which has often resulted in huge numbers of job losses, may have led to a significant change of attitude towards fraud in the workplace," observes the head of fraud investigations at KPMG Forensic.[11]

Yet managers address some ethical dilemmas by looking beyond the company's self-interest or the minimum legal requirements. Consider the situation that the pharmaceutical giant Merck faced when its scientists discovered that ivermectin, one of its drugs, might be used for treating river blindness. At the time, this disease afflicted an estimated 18 million people in less-developed nations. Merck's executives realized that perfecting a form of ivermectin for this purpose would be costly and would bring in little or no revenue. However, the CEO encouraged company scientists to move ahead because the drug could potentially benefit so many people. Then, realizing that no system existed for delivering ivermectin to the areas where it was needed, the company also created a suitable distribution system. In this instance, Merck's managers went well beyond the firm's immediate self-interest and legal obligations to take actions they considered to be ethical—despite the $200 million cost for making and distributing the drug during the first decade alone.[12]

Increased globalization has also complicated the ethical decisions faced by companies that cross borders to buy, produce, or sell goods and services.[13] Multinational firms often have managers from diverse backgrounds and cultures and do business in different geographic locations governed by different laws and customs. The resulting variations in values, languages, regulations, and traditions complicate the decision-making process about ethical issues that multinationals confront.

Technology plays a role, as well. In recent years, much attention has focused on the ethical issues raised by the use of Internet technology for sales, research, distribution, promotion, communication, recruiting, and other business-related tasks.[14] For example, consumers worry about misuse of *cookies*—small amounts of data that Web sites store on an Internet user's computer. What kind of information is being collected, by what types of sites, from what types of users? Who sees and uses the data—and for what purposes? Should consumers be allowed to edit or even delete personal information that Web sites gather? Should data be collected from children? U.S. legislators have addressed some of these ethical issues. To illustrate, the Children's Online Privacy Protection Act requires Web sites to get parental consent before collecting or disclosing data collected from children under 13 years old. However, other issues relating to electronic commerce are still being hotly debated by consumers and consumer advocates, businesses, and regulatory agencies, putting ethics in the spotlight as the Internet's reach expands.

In addition, scandals such as the financial shenanigans at Enron have raised public awareness of ethical lapses and prompted investigations, hearings, and even new laws. From Capitol Hill to Wall Street to Main Street, people reacted to the bankruptcies and ongoing disclosures of corporate missteps by talking of executive "villains" and calling for harsher penalties, including jail time for white-collar criminals.[15] The Sarbanes-Oxley Act now requires the CEOs of all publicly traded U.S. corporations to swear to the accuracy and completeness of the major financial reports they file with the SEC—or face prosecution and prison time. When this requirement became effective in August, 2002, some companies decided to restate their financial reports before their CEOs certified the results. The consumer finance firm Household

International, for example, revealed that its earnings since 1994 had been overstated by $386 million.[16]

Examining Contemporary Ethical Challenges

When confronted with an ethical challenge, managers should start by examining the facts. What exactly is happening, and what are the decision options for the organization? Managers should also think through the probable outcomes of each potential decision. What is likely to happen as a result of each decision option—and how will the consequences affect the company, its customers, and other groups connected with the organization?[17]

Managers can apply a variety of approaches for resolving ethical issues in business. The *utilitarian approach* suggests that the most ethical decision is the one that produces the greatest good (and the least harm) for the greatest number of people. The *rights approach* suggests that decisions be evaluated on the basis of whether they respect or violate the rights of the people who will be affected. The *fairness approach* (also known as the *justice approach*) suggests evaluating each decision on the basis if whether it unfairly discriminates against someone or results in favoritism toward someone. The *common-good approach* suggests managers look more broadly at how their decisions affect the common good of society overall (as Merck's CEO did when he decided to move ahead with the drug to treat river blindness). The *virtue approach* suggests that managers, as members of society, make decisions that uphold virtues such as honesty, compassion, and fairness.

In practice, managers confronted with ethical issues can apply these approaches by asking five key questions:

1. What good and harm are likely to come out of each decision option, and which option is likely to result in the most beneficial outcome overall?

2. Who is affected by each decision option and which option shows the most respect for the rights of these people?

3. Which decision option most effectively avoids unfair discrimination or favoritism?

4. Which decision option most effectively contributes to the common good?

5. Which decision option most effectively upholds positive virtues?

As these questions demonstrate, ethical managers must consider how their decisions will affect other people inside and outside the organization. The next section describes the groups that managers generally consider when weighing the outcomes of their decisions and actions.

STAKEHOLDER RELATIONS

One common theme running through the ethical challenges described earlier in this chapter is that some individuals or groups—customers, employees, or others—are likely to be hurt while others are helped in some way as a result of the company's decisions. As noted earlier, Merck's decision to develop and distribute its drug to combat river blindness helped millions of people around the world. At the same time, however, it reduced the profits available for distribution to Merck's shareholders and workforce.

How do companies approach ethical challenges from the viewpoint of managing relations with these different stakeholders? *Stakeholders* are people or groups who have a stake in the company, either because they can be influenced by what it does to achieve its objectives or because they can influence its ability to achieve those objectives.[18] As the Merck example shows, many ethical challenges come about because companies are trying to balance the often conflicting demands and expectations of different stakeholders.[19]

In general, companies are influenced by or exert influence on a number of stakeholder groups, including employees, owners and shareholders, customers, suppliers, the community, and other stakeholders.[20]

Employees as Stakeholders

Employees at all levels are the lifeblood of the organization, making and implementing the decisions that keep companies functioning and successful. Beyond simply earning a living, they have different expectations of the company, ranging from job stability and empowerment to the opportunity to do meaningful work. Yet many stand to lose their jobs—and sometimes their pensions and other benefits—when top managers or others inside the organization follow questionable ethical paths. Conversely, ethical companies can more easily recruit employees. In one national survey, 80 percent of the employees who said their managers would upheld ethical standards were willing to refer others as job candidates.[21] However, many top executives receive multi-million dollar salaries and bonuses far in excess of the typical employee's compensation. How are companies responsible to employees as stakeholders, and vice versa?

Consider what happened when Nike was criticized for labor practices at the overseas factories that make its shoes and apparel. After months of negative publicity, Nike established a code of conduct for labor practices—one of the first by a U.S. company—and began auditing its worldwide factories for compliance. Management knew that the controversy's effect on customers was a major issue, but also recognized that Nike's U.S. employees were directly affected by the uproar. "The way it hurt our business was that it hurt our people," said a Nike vice president. "Individual employees at Nike started to wonder what kind of company they were working for and what message was being sent about the people who worked there."[22]

Owners and Shareholders as Stakeholders

Owners include the entrepreneurs and small businesspeople who own their own companies as well as the investors who buy shares in publicly-traded corporations. These stakeholders may demand much more than a chance to enjoy financial returns on their investments. Some may ask a company to provide jobs for family members or friends; others may expect a company to be a good corporate citizen or to demonstrate innovation and leadership.

Ethically, what does the company owe its owners and shareholders? In the case of Enron and other corporations accused of manipulating the figures to make financial results look better, are top executives responsible for ensuring that shareholders receive full and accurate disclosure of finances and risks? Enron, for example, reported hundreds of millions of dollars in profits even as one of its many partnerships—specifically designed to shift risks—experienced heavy losses. If Enron had not used improper accounting techniques to hide the problems and had released a highly detailed balance sheet when reporting results, shareholders would have known much earlier about the company's weakening financial situation. Instead, shareholders who held onto their stock saw the share price fall until all shareholder value was wiped out by Enron's bankruptcy within a matter of months.[23]

Customers as Stakeholders

Customers are vital stakeholders because they provide the revenue that allows companies to reach their profit goals. However, companies do not always act in the best interests of their customers, as some of the earlier examples indicate. What rights and responsibilities do companies owe their customers, and vice versa? How much influence on corporate affairs should customers have? Are some customers (such as those who buy more frequently or in larger volume) entitled to preferential treatment? Should management consider customers more important than employees, shareholders, and other stakeholders?

Firestone faced an ethical challenge several years ago when the National Highway Traffic Safety Administration ordered a recall of the tires it had sold for sport-utility vehicles such as the Ford Explorer. The agency attributed more than 200 deaths to tread separation on the Firestone tires. Firestone agreed to recall 6.5 million tires but publicly fought the government's attempt to expand the recall, saying its other tires were not defective. Meanwhile, Ford emphasized customer safety by voluntarily replacing 13 million Firestone tires for its customers. Ultimately, Firestone agreed to recall almost 1 million more tires that the agency declared defective. Still, the months of delay and battles with Ford over responsibility hurt the company's image among customers.[24]

Suppliers as Stakeholders

Suppliers seek a mutually-beneficial arrangement with the companies to which they sell goods and services. They want to work with companies that will continue to buy year in and year out and, if possible, they seek to increase the size and frequency of customer orders over the years. Giant corporations often request special services and other extras, and many suppliers go to great lengths to accommodate these valued customers. Yet what do companies actually owe suppliers as stakeholders?

The problem is compounded when a huge buyer such as WorldCom declares bankruptcy, suspending payments to large and small suppliers alike. Before the bankruptcy, the ServiceMaster One Call janitorial service in Flowood, Mississippi, had assigned 40 employees every day to clean WorldCom's headquarters in Clinton, Mississippi. Afterward, owner Steve Warner worried about receiving the $20,000 that WorldCom owed him. ServiceMaster was far from alone: WorldCom owed $300 million to SBC Communications and $183 million to Verizon, as just two examples among many. "WorldCom is so big, you have to keep it alive to sustain other industries," observed one telecommunications supplier.[25]

Communities as Stakeholders

The decisions and actions of companies can affect communities in a variety of ways. When companies create or eliminate jobs, they have an economic effect on local communities. The taxes they pay are important sources of revenue for communities. Also, companies affect the environment through their use of natural resources and the way their operations pollute or protect ecological conditions. And they can influence the quality of life within the community through charitable donations, support for the arts, and other programs. In turn, cities and states frequently make special arrangements to attract and retain businesses, such as allowing companies tax credits in exchange for creating jobs. From an ethical perspective, what are a company's responsibilities to its community?

The WorldCom bankruptcy hurt many communities that were expecting to collect taxes, cable fees, and other payments. It also left some charities and nonprofits with large budget gaps. MarcoPolo, a Web-based program that shows teachers how to use online resources in the classroom, received $50 million in funding from WorldCom and its MCI unit during the five years before the bankruptcy. The program had to scramble for new sources of funding after WorldCom went bankrupt.[26]

Other Stakeholders

Taking a broader view, groups such as government regulators, legislators, the media, the supplier's employees and suppliers, trade associations, political groups, and even competitors can be considered stakeholders because they are either affected by or can affect the company's performance. And some companies take the stakeholder concept a step further.

In London, the Co-operative Bank identifies seven stakeholder groups it calls *partners*: shareholders, customers, suppliers, the local community, employees and their families, future generations of customers, and national/international society. To measure its performance in meeting these partners' demands and expectations, the bank uses three measures: value created for each partner, ability to deliver the expected value, and effectiveness in socially-responsible value delivery.[27] Because each stakeholder group generally has different needs, expectations, and concerns, the Co-operative Bank, like other companies, faces difficult ethical decisions in trying to balance the conflicting interests of its stakeholders.

Balancing Stakeholders' Interests

The Co-operative Bank's experience illustrates the delicate balancing act with which all company managers must contend. "Our 3,800 suppliers want to be paid quickly, treated fairly," notes the bank's corporate affairs manager. "Our families want to make sure that their mum or dad gets home from work on time and doesn't work late. As a result of partners wanting different things, there are conflicts of interest. It isn't some perfect world. There are situations where giving to one partner means taking away from another. That is why trying to achieve the best

balance over time is the aim of the partnership approach of the bank."[28]

How can managers make ethical decisions that balance the conflicting interests of these

groups without disgruntling some or all? Research suggests that stakeholders tend to be satisfied

and understanding when managers use timeliness, honesty, and empathy to communicate their

decisions.[29] Even when a decision does not satisfy the expectations of a particular stakeholder

group, the company can preserve good relations by demonstrating empathy and concern,

presenting details honestly, and communicating in a timely manner so all stakeholders are aware

of the decision, the reasoning, and the outcome.

Companies generally place the highest priority on relations with three stakeholder groups

in particular: shareholders, employees, and customers. These three groups are the most directly

affected by or can most directly affect company performance. Their demands and interests are

not always aligned, however, creating a tricky balancing act and ethical challenges for managers.

Dealing with Shareholders

Honesty in dealing with shareholders has become a major issue in recent years. Clearly,

shareholders have a right to expect accurate, complete, and understandable financial reports from

the companies in which they invest. Yet many observers believe that the revelations about

suspect financial reporting by Enron, WorldCom, and other companies have shaken investor

confidence. WorldCom's investors saw the share price dive from a 1999 high of $64.50 to 9

cents at the time of its bankruptcy filing in mid-2002, after the company admitted improperly

accounting for billions of dollars in expenses in an attempt to report higher profits. Investors are unlikely to wring any value out of their shares if and when the company is able to reorganize and emerge from bankruptcy.[30]

Moreover, revelations about securities analysts being pressured by their employers to continue recommending certain stocks have also hurt investor confidence. New York's attorney general has pushed Wall Street firms to adopt new rules preventing their investment bankers (who usher new stock offerings to market) from improperly pressuring their analysts (who research company finances and issue reports about the stock's prospects).[31] Regulators are also investigating banking behemoths such as Citigroup and J.P. Morgan Chase for their role in questionable transactions that helped Enron and other investment banking clients hide debt and shape their financial results in other ways.[32] Some of the public pension funds that invested in WorldCom's $11.8 billion bond issue in 2001—and suffered huge losses in 2002—sued the banks that handled the bond offering (as well as the company and its former top executives). They alleged that the defendants should have known about WorldCom's true financial situation, a charge the banks deny.[33]

A growing number of shareholders are paying closer attention to the social responsibility actions of the companies in which they invest. In response, McDonald's and other companies are releasing sustainability reports, showing how their business operations affect the environment, human rights, and other social issues. Royal Dutch/Shell now includes its sustainability report with its annual report so shareholders can read about the company's financial and social responsibility performance at the same time. Some companies even have their social responsibility reports audited, to increase confidence among shareholders.[34]

Another concern revolves around how public companies report information about the cost of the *stock options* they grant to some or all employees. These options, given as a reward for performance, allow (but do not require) the employees to buy the company's stock at a certain price during a certain period. Over time, if the stock price goes up, the employees can exercise their options to buy at the older, lower price. Then, as the stock price appreciates, the employees profit and remain motivated to continue their outstanding performance. Different companies use stock options in different ways. Ford, for example, awards stock options only to top-performing managers, less than 10 percent of its 350,000 workforce. In contrast, Amazon.com has granted some options to nearly every one of its 7,700 employees.[35]

The way companies account for these options—not the options themselves—are the issue. In the past, most companies mentioned options in footnotes to their financial reports, with little explanation. Now, in the spirit of more transparency, General Electric, Cola-Cola, and other companies are treating stock options as another expense to be more fully disclosed in financial reports, along with rent and other expenses. Many companies that announced this more straightforward method of disclosing the cost of options have been rewarded by higher share prices, indicating that shareholders applaud their honesty.[36]

The balancing act with stock options comes in when employees wind up being hurt due to the trend toward more complete disclosure to shareholders. This is because reporting options as an expense makes the corporate bottom line look a little thinner. As a result, some companies may curtail their use of stock options and seek other methods to motivate and reward the workforce—methods that less directly affect the earnings figures they report quarterly and annually. Amazon.com, for example, is changing its reward program to move away from options while continuing to stress share ownership, in some form, as a motivating factor for employees.[37] Is it ethical for companies to change or eliminate a valuable employee benefit because of a move toward more transparent accounting?

Dealing with Employees

Employees and managers have a right to expect equitable rewards for their performance, as well as honesty and integrity from their employers. Yet cultivating an internal atmosphere of trust can be difficult as companies struggle with shareholders' demands for immediate financial performance, among other pressures. Seeking to cut labor costs and boost financial results, many U.S. airlines laid off employees and pushed hard for union give-backs during the yearlong travel slump that followed the terrorist attacks on New York City and Washington, D.C. in 2001. An overall economic slowdown during the same period prompted other companies to lay off workers and search for other ways to slash costs.

On the one hand, how can companies continue operating with the same costs when revenues drop and remain low for many months? On the other hand, how can employees keep believing in employers who may eliminate their jobs with little or no advance warning? As one WorldCom employee said after the company's bankruptcy, "we worked and gave the company everything. I don't think anyone personally feels guilty, but there's a sense of disappointment. It impacts everyone. Morale suffers when these kinds of things happen."[38]

Among the numerous ethical issues that concern employees are compensation, benefits, and retirement programs; the growing disparity between management and employee pay packages; and severance pay and job security. Consider the situation at Electronic Data Systems (EDS), which acquired the travel technology firm Sabre along with the employees of all its units. EDS promised that if it laid off any Sabre workers within a year of initiating a severance agreement after the acquisition, it would pay them one month's salary plus up to one month's pay for each year they had been with Sabre. During that year, EDS saw one of its largest customers and suppliers (WorldCom) go bankrupt and learned it would have to conduct an expensive round of extra testing for a giant government project it was handling.

Just one day after the agreement expired, EDS laid off 300 of the former Sabre employees as well as 1,700 non-Sabre employees. That single day made a huge difference in severance pay. An account manager who had worked for Sabre for nine years expected to receive only $3,000 in severance pay, compared with $68,000 he would have received if laid off a day earlier. The laid-off employees protested and some joined class-action lawsuits against EDS. An EDS spokesperson said, "The former Sabre employees were treated the same way as the 1,700 other EDS'ers that were affected; there's a personal story behind each of those 2,000 EDS employees. The Sabre employees were not targeted."[39] Was this decision ethical?

Another issue is protecting the assets held in employees' pension funds and 401(k) retirement plans. Often companies use stock rather than cash to fund their employees' pensions and retirement plans—and force employees to retain the contributed stock for an extended period. (At Enron, for example, employees could not sell company-contributed stock until they turned 50 years old.) Over time, company stock may account for half or more of the retirement plan's assets—creating a huge risk for employees if the stock value drops. Risk became reality at Lucent Technologies and other companies, where a sharp decrease in share price hurt the retirement holdings of thousands of workers.[40] Were the companies acting ethically when they chose to contribute stock rather than cash and prevented employees from selling their shares until it was too late to prevent devastating losses?

Employees who lose their jobs when scandal-ridden companies go bust also worry about being stigmatized for having worked there. "If you've been at a WorldCom or Enron or any other company that's imploded, there's a mark against you," observes an executive recruiter in

Cleveland. "You can very easily get to a position of no hope." A consultant who formerly worked for Enron confirms, "There are some people who refuse to hire anyone with Enron on their résumé. People have put 'major energy company' on their profiles so they can get past that hurdle and in the door." Laid-off employees are reacting by commiserating on Web sites, filing lawsuits, and pushing for legislative reform to prevent recurrences.[41] From the employee's perspective, what are the ethics of omitting employers' names from a résumé? From the company's perspective, what are the ethics of eliminating a job candidate from consideration simply because he or she worked for a company embroiled in scandal?

To avoid allowing ill will to poison relations between employers and employees, human resources experts recommend conducting a periodic climate survey to gauge employee morale and attitudes. This not only demonstrates empathy, it keeps communication lines open and—if management acts on the results—offers opportunities for strengthening ties with the entire workforce. Stratus Technologies, a high-tech firm based in Massachusetts, uses a 50-question climate survey to find out more about its employees' concerns. One year, "we discovered that there was considerable dissatisfaction within one functional area around our stock option program," remembers the company's top human resources executive. "When we looked again at how they were being granted to those employees, we found some inequities, which we then corrected." [42]

Surveys can also bring out concerns about certain managers and work groups. At the same time, Stratus and other companies can build trust by letting employees know that management will review and weigh every comment on the surveys, then decide on what action to take after considering the potential consequences for all stakeholders. However, is it ethical for a company to conduct a climate survey with no intention of responding to employees' concerns or implementing changes?

Dealing with Customers

Companies cannot exist without the trust and patronage of their customers. At the same time, *caveat emptor*—let the buyer beware—remains many a customer's attitude in light of the recent scandals that have rocked the business world. The antidote to customer suspicion? Management must find ways to earn and keep the trust of their customers over the long term. Building a reputation for ethical decisions can go a long way toward building trust among customers.

Nonetheless, when things go wrong, many companies initially try to deny or deflect responsibility, contributing to the crisis in customer confidence. Instead, experts stress the importance of quickly acknowledging the problem and publicly issuing a sincere, clear apology. America West Airlines, for example, made headlines not long ago because two of its pilots were accused of preparing to fly a plane while apparently under the influence of alcohol. Months later, a passenger was removed from an America West flight after she joked about the airline's pilots. The *Today Show* invited the passenger and an America West executive to discuss the incident on national television. Rather than trying to explain or excuse the airline's behavior, the executive stated, "I'm here primarily to apologize . . . We overreacted." The passenger responded by saying, "I appreciate the apology. I'm sympathetic to America West right now. I know they're going through a tough time."[43]

Companies rarely deal with all customers in exactly the same way. In part, the differences reflect different purchasing volumes and related service costs. But companies sometimes face decisions about pricing and other issues that are driven more by marketing or financial priorities, leading to ethical questions. For instance, Cingular and Verizon, among other wireless telephone service providers, are promoting prepaid plans to less credit-worthy customers at higher per-minute charges than those paid by customers with better credit histories.[44] Is it ethical to set higher prices for less credit-worthy customers who often have lower incomes than more credit-worthy customers?

For their part, customer groups who disagree with a company's decisions sometimes use boycotts and other campaigns to promote change through financial pressure, public embarrassment, and other methods. As one example, the National Council of Women's Organizations called on Coca-Cola and other sponsors of the Masters Tournament to pressure the Augusta National Golf Club to admit female members; it also asked CBS not to air the event. The group might have boycotted the sponsors' products if the companies refused to withdraw their support of the tournament until the golf club allowed women members. Considering that women buy 80 percent of all U.S. consumer products, an effective boycott could have hurt these companies' sales and reputations. Although Coca-Cola held talks with the council, the Augusta National Golf Club responded by dropping the tournament's corporate sponsors to relieve the pressure on them.[45] Is it ethical for corporate sponsors to support an organization or event seen as discriminatory by a sizable customer group? From the companies' perspective, is it ethical for customers to exert this kind of pressure?

Chapter 2 examines a number of ethical issues confronting companies today and looks at how management can support and encourage ethical decisions and actions throughout the organization.

QUESTIONS FOR REVIEW

1. What is business ethics?

2. How do ethical dilemmas differ from ethical lapses?

3. Why are ethical decisions in the best interest of a company?

4. What are some of the pressures complicating the ethical decisions faced by managers today?

5. What are the five approaches a manager may apply when confronted with an ethical challenge?

6. Identify a company's most important stakeholder groups.

7. Why do companies face ethical issues when they try to satisfy more than one stakeholder group?

8. What does GAAP stand for?

REFERENCES

_____

1. Andrew Backover, "Pressure to Perform Felt as Problems Hit," *USA Today,* July 1, 2002, www.usatoday.com.

2. John A. Byrne, "After Enron: The Ideal Corporation," *Business Week,* August 26, 2002, pp. 68-74; Kurt Eichenwald and Diana B. Henriques, "Enron Buffed Image to a Shine Even as It Rotted from Within," *New York Times,* February 10, 2002, pp. 1, 28-29; Daniel McGinn, "The Ripple Effect," *Newsweek,* February 18, 2002, pp. 29+.

3. John A. Byrne, "Fall From Grace," *Business Week,* August 12, 2002, pp. 50-56; "Corporate Accountability," *Wall Street Journal*, August 6, 2002, www.wsj.com.

4. Herb Greenberg, "Legal—But Lousy," *Fortune,* September 2, 2002, p. 192; Jared Sandberg and Susan Pulliam, "WorldCom Finds More Errors; Restatement Will Be $7.2 Billion," *Wall Street Journal*, August 9, 2002, www.wsj.com; Barnaby J. Feder and Seth Schiesel, "WorldCom Finds $3.3 Billion More in Irregularities," *New York Times,* August 9, 2002, www.nytimes.com.

5. Devin Leonard, "The Adelphia Story," *Fortune,* August 12, 2002, p. 164-148; Richard A. Oppel Jr., "Chief Acknowledges 'Debate' on Global Crossing Deals," *New York Times,* March 22, 2002, pp. C4+.

6. "A Whiff of Impropriety," *The Economist,* August 3, 2002, pp. 54-55.

7. Adapted from John R. Boatright, *Ethics and the Conduct of Business 4th ed.* (Upper Saddle River, N.J.: Prentice Hall, 2003), chapter 1.

8. Boatright, *Ethics and the Conduct of Business,* p. 18.

9. This section draws, in part, on material in Michael H. Mescon, Courtland L. Boveé, and John V. Thill, *Business Today 10th ed.* (Upper Saddle River, N.J.: Prentice Hall, 2003), p. 44.

10. Thomas I. White, "Resolving an Ethical Dilemma," (n.d.), www.ethicsandbursiness.org.

11. "Most Staff Would Report Office Fraudsters to Bosses," *Personnel Today,* September 17, 2002, p. 7.

12. N. Craig Smith, "Ethical Guidelines for Marketing Practice: A Reply to Gaski and some Observations on the Role of Normative Marketing Ethics," *Journal of Business Ethics* 23 (2001): pp. 3-18; Sidney Goldstein, "Tales of Corporate Altruism," *Family Practice News,* June 1, 2001, p. 9.

13. "Managing Business Ethics to Prevent and Detect Fraud in the Global Marketplace," *IOMA's Report on Preventing Business Fraud,* Institute of Management and Administration, November 2001, pp. 2-5.

14. Bette Ann Stead and Jackie Gilbert, "Ethical Issues in Electronic Commerce," *Journal of Business Ethics* 34 (2001): pp. 75-85.

15. Clifton Leaf, "Enough Is Enough: White-Collar Criminals," *Fortune,* March 18, 2002, pp. 60+; Jonathan D. Glater, "Mad As Hell: Hard Time for White-Collar Crime," *New York Times,* July 28, 2002, sec. 4, p. 5.

16. Michael Schroeder, "Under the Gun from the SEC, Firms Divulge Accounting Issues," *Wall Street Journal*, August 15, 2002, pp. 1+.

17. This section draws, in part, on Manuel Valesquez, Claire Andre, Thomas Shanks, and Michael J. Meyer, "Thinking Ethically: A Framework for Moral Decision Making," in John E. Richardson ed., *Business Ethics 14 ed. 2002-2003* (Guilford, CT: McGraw-Hill/Dushkin, 2002), pp. 2-4; and Ricky W. Griffin and Ronald J. Ebert, *Business 6th ed.* (Upper Saddle River, N.J.: Prentice Hall, 2002), chap. 4.

18. Boatright, *Ethics and the Conduct of Business,* pp. 390-391.

19. S. Venkataraman, "Stakeholder Value Equilibration and the Entrepreneurial Process," in R. Edward Freeman and Sankaran Venkataraman, eds., *Ethics and Entrepreneurship* (Charlottesville, VA: Society for Business Ethics, 2002), pp. 45-57.

20. The following sections draw, in part, on material in Sandra Waddock, "Comments on 'Stakeholder Value Equilibration and the Entrepreneurial Process,' by S. Venkataraman," in R. Edward Freeman and Sankaran Venkataraman, eds., *Ethics and Entrepreneurship* (Charlottesville, VA: Society for Business Ethics, 2002), pp. 163-173.

21. Thomas Donaldson, "The Corporate Ethics Boom: Significant or Just for Show?" *Financial Times Mastering Management*, November 13, 2000, knowledge.wharton.upenn.edu/articles.cfm?articleid=285&catid=11.

22. Dean Williams, "Weaving Ethics Into Corporate Culture," *Communication World*, June-July 2002, pp. 38+; Tania Mason, "Nike Axes 'Sweatshop' After BBC Investigation," *Marketing*, October 19, 2000, p. 5; Roger Parloff, "Can We Talk?" *Fortune*, September 2, 2002, pp. 102-110.

23. Eichenwald and Henriques, "Enron Buffed Image to a Shine."

24. Harry Stoffer, "Firestone Surrenders as Hard-Line Strategy Fails," *Automotive News*, October 8, 2001, p. 1.

25. Jon Swartz, "WorldCom Woes Ripple Through Economies," *USA Today*, August 9, 2002, www.usatoday.com.

26. Swartz, "WorldCom Woes Ripple Through Economies."

27. Trevor Phillips, Bill Eyres, and Richard Howitt, "Closing Session—The Corporation and Society," *Journal of Business Ethics* 32 (2001): pp. 119-126.

28. Phillips, Eyres, and Howitt, "Closing Session—The Corporation and Society."

29. Kelly C. Strong, Richard C. Ringer, and Steven A. Taylor, "THE Rules of Stakeholder Satisfaction (Timeliness, Honesty, Empathy)," *Journal of Business Ethics* 32 (2001): pp. 219-230.

30. Andrew Backover, "WorldCom Files for Chapter 11 Protection," *USA Today,* July 22, 2002, www.usatoday.com.

31. Gretchen Morgenson, "Pressuring Analysts: Hard Habit to Break," *New York Times,* August 11, 2002, sec. 3, pp. 1, 14-15.

32. Julie Creswell, "Banks on the Hot Seat," *Fortune,* September 2, 2002, pp. 79-82.

33. Paul Beckett and Jathon Sapsford, "California Pension Funds' Lawsuit Alleges Bond Fraud by WorldCom," *Wall Street Journal*, July 17, 2002, www.wsj.com.

34. Amy Cortese, "The New Accountability: Tracking the Social Costs," *New York Times,* March 24, 2002, sec. 3, p. 4.

35. Jeff D. Opdyke and Michelle Higgins, "Workers to Bear Brunt of Push for Firms to Expense Options," *Wall Street Journal*, August 7, 2002, www.wsj.com.

36. David Stires, "A Little Honesty Goes a Long Way," *Fortune,* September 2, 2002, p. 186; Opdyke and Higgins, "Workers to Bear Brunt of Push;" Allan Sloan, "How to Look Like a Good Guy," *Newsweek,* August 12, 2002, p. 32.

37. Opdyke and Higgins, "Workers to Bear Brunt of Push."

38. Stephanie Armour, "Laid-Off Workers Still Feel Fallout," *USA Today,* August 1, 2002, www.usatoday.com.

39. Jennifer Bayot, "Timing of EDS Layoffs Proved Costly to Workers," *New York Times,* July 28, 2002, sec. 3, p. 6.

40. Ellen E. Schultz, "Should Pension Law Do More for Workers?" *Wall Street Journal*, January 14, 2002, p. A8.

41. Armour, "Laid-Off Workers Still Feel Fallout."

42. Liz Simpson, "What's Going On In Your Company?" *Training,* June 2002, pp. 30-34.

43. Mike France, "The Mea Culpa Defense," *Business Week,* August 26, 2002, pp. 76-78.

44. Stephanie N. Mehta, "Is There Any Way Out of the Telecom Mess?" *Fortune,* July 22, 2002, pp. 82+.

45. Toddi Gutner, "More Heat on the Masters," *Business Week,* August 12, 2002, p. 75; Scott Leith, "Coke Tried to Cool Off Masters Fight Behind Scenes," *Atlanta Journal-Constitution,* September 4, 2002, p. A1; Glenn Sheeley, "Women's Group Warns CBS Not to Air Masters," *Atlanta Journal-Constitution,* September 1, 2002, p. A1.

Chapter 2: Key Issues in Contemporary Business Ethics

Management Responsibility

    Accountability and Control

    Corporate Culture

    Conflicts of Interest

    Legal Compliance

    Insider Trading

Corporate Governance

    Composition of the Board

    Role of the Audit Committee

    Role of Stakeholders

Accounting Practices

    Following GAAP

        Handling Expenses and Revenues

        Taking A New Look at Old Practices

    Working with Auditors

        Auditing and Consulting

        Checks on Auditors

Ethical Decisions and Behavior

    Codes of Conduct

    Ethics Training

    Whistleblowers

MANAGEMENT RESPONSIBILITY

Senior managers play three broad roles within a company. First, they are responsible for making economic decisions that lead to profitability and other financial goals. Second, they serve as trustees of company assets and are expected to take actions that benefit owners and shareholders (and often other stakeholders). Third, their power as senior corporate officials allows them to interact in significant ways with legal and regulatory bodies and to demonstrate corporate leadership in dealing with key societal concerns.[1] As a result, top managers are responsible for personally making ethical decisions and ensuring that other managers and employees make ethical decisions in line with corporate goals and good stakeholder relations.

Yet many recent business scandals can be traced to the questionable decisions and actions of top management. The chief financial officer (CFO), for example, has traditionally been responsible for directing the company's financial management activities, including overseeing the completion of accurate financial reports for shareholders and regulators. At one time, many CFOs were Certified Public Accountants (CPAs) trained in public accounting practices and familiar with the applicable laws and guidelines governing corporate finance. Today, however, only 20 percent of the CFOs at *Fortune* 500 firms are CPAs, whereas 35 percent have M.B.A. degrees (5 percent have both qualifications). In recent decades, the CFO also has become involved in strategic planning and in designing complex financial transactions to support company goals and strategies. *The Economist* magazine, noting these trends, recently referred to the CFO as the "chief fiddling officer" for dealing with relentless pressure for profitability by managing earnings in more creative ways.[2]

Accountability and Control

The arrests of WorldCom's former CFO Scott Sullivan and former controller David Myers on securities fraud charges, only a few weeks after the company declared bankruptcy, signaled that excessive creativity will no longer be tolerated. According to the charges, the two executives directed subordinates to improperly book certain *operating expenses* (short-term expenses related to daily operations, which are supposed to be deducted from current income) as *capital expenses* (major expenses such as certain product development costs, which can be deducted in smaller amounts over a longer period). This effectively improved the earnings that WorldCom showed on its income statement.

Sullivan reportedly received $45 million in bonuses and stock options from WorldCom during 1999 through 2002. If he is convicted, he may be required to give up some or all of these assets. Until then, he is allowed to use his funds as he chooses. However, under the Sarbanes-Oxley Act, which took effect as of August, 2002, CEOs and CFOs now will be forced to return their compensation if their companies have to restate their financial reports due to "misconduct." This anti-fraud bill also outlaws most company loans to top executives, largely because some are never repaid.[3]

Little more than a month after the former WorldCom executives were taken into custody, the founder of Adelphia Communications and two of his sons were arrested and charged with using corporate funds for personal gain. More management arrests and indictments are expected, as President Bush, Congress, the Justice Department, and the SEC promised vigorous action to combat corporate fraud. The goal is to hold senior managers more accountable for suspect and illegal decisions and activities.[4]

Some observers see greed as a primary motivation behind senior managers' missteps. "That extreme greed at the top is new," observes management expert Peter Drucker, "and what it has done is to destroy the trust of operating management in top management." Federal Reserve Board Chairman Alan Greenspan also speaks of "infectious greed" gripping U.S. businesses. In fact, many executive pay packages are staggeringly outsized but become effective only when the company achieves certain performance targets—a difficult temptation for some to resist. To rein in greedy actions, the Sarbanes-Oxley Act states that senior managers who knowingly certify misleading financial statements can be jailed and fined up to $5 million. Destroying or changing records to thwart a federal investigation will also lead to jail time, as will actions designed to defraud investors. [5]

A related issue is pressure to keep performance at consistently high levels for long periods. The coauthor of *What Went Wrong at Enron* comments that Enron's method of ranking the performance of all employees twice a year, then letting the bottom 15 percent go was "quite extreme," leading to a "dysfunctional organization." Under former CEO Kenneth Lay, Enron lacked strong management controls: "Rather than having central guidance, things were set up as a free-for-all," he notes. [6] The executive director of the Center for Business Ethics at Bentley College stresses: "In this competitive, capitalistic system of ours, of course you have to have financial targets and goals that keep you pointed in the right economic and competitive direction. But you've also got to tell employees you can only meet those goals within the framework of our ethical values." Although Lay and other top managers at scandal-ridden companies say they were unaware of the extent and nature of their firms' missteps, one academic expert sums up the reaction of many observers: "I don't think it's an adequate defense for a CEO to say, 'How could I know everything that's going on?' It doesn't absolve them of responsibility." [7]

Corporate Culture

In part, the ethical problems encountered by Enron and other corporate high-flyers may have been linked to their relative youth as business entities. Why? "A longstanding company has usually developed a corporate culture that restrains an aggressive CEO from getting out of control," observes business historian Professor Richard Sylla.[8]

Yet Xerox, hardly a corporate newcomer, also has admitted "improper payments" by an international unit and is investigating potential accounting irregularities in other international units. The company's assistant treasurer said he was part of a group that helped the company overstate profits by $1.4 billion from 1997 to 2001. "Sometimes I fed the beast," he told the press. "The beast was a Xerox culture that created an illusion of value."[9]

The CEO is perhaps the most important influence on corporate culture. "Once you as CEO go over the line," the CEO of Unisys told an audience of U.S. executives, "then people think it's okay to go over the line themselves." For disgraced firms trying to battle back from scandal or bankruptcy, a major challenge is "finding replacement CEOs who are above reproach yet still able to lead companies back from the depths," according to a major executive recruiting firm.[10] Pressure from the top can lead other executives to make suspect decisions. In one survey of CFOs, 17 percent said that CEOs had exerted pressure to have financial results misrepresented during the past five years—and 5 percent said they had done so, violating GAAP (generally accepted accounting principles) in the process.[11] Without strong, respectable leaders, how can companies set high standards for ethical conduct that will permeate the organization's culture?

Some corporate leaders are taking a stand against the pressure to report ever-higher revenues and profits. When James Kilts became CEO of Gillette, he met with securities analysts who were seeking guidance about the firm's projected future earnings. Instead of announcing more aggressive financial targets, in the manner of many incoming CEOs, he denounced the company's earlier forecasts as unrealistically high and then refused to make any new earnings predictions. Breaking with tradition, United Technologies has also begun issuing more conservative earnings targets, despite the grumblings of securities analysts.[12] Should firms publicly commit to ambitious financial goals that may encourage unethical decisions and actions?

Another example of the CEO's influence on company-wide ethics comes from CenterBeam, a California firm that installs wireless Web-connected computer systems for small companies. Growing fast, CenterBeam had interviewed and offered a position to a qualified job candidate. Before that candidate had a chance to respond, the company received a résumé from an even more outstanding applicant. This created a dilemma: Should the company revoke its offer to the first candidate in order to hire the second? The CEO never hesitated: "We made a promise to the first candidate," he stated. "If we're going to be the kind of company that people trust, we've got to keep our promises."[13]

Conflicts of Interest

In business, a *conflict of interest* occurs when the personal interests of managers or employees interfere with their obligation to make decisions and take actions that are in the best interests of the company's stakeholders. Often ethical questions arise when management must choose between taking actions that benefit themselves and taking actions that benefit investors, customers, employees, or other stakeholder groups.

Consider just a few of the conflicts of interest at Enron. Andrew Fastow, the former CFO, set up complicated partnerships to remove specific assets and liabilities from Enron's books—

partnerships that benefited Fastow and select other Enron executives and investors. The company's code of conduct outlawed such conflicts of interest, but the board of directors exempted Fastow from complying with the rules. In fact, Merrill Lynch's investment prospectus for one of the partnerships noted, "A. Fastow's dual role creates advantages for the fund and Enron." This disclosure dissuaded many institutions from investing, although Citigroup and J.P. Morgan Chase were not deterred. When the conflict came to light, a former SEC chairman commented: "The CFO is the financial conscience of the company, the guardian of the numbers. If he has a conflict, how can the system work?"[14]

Some of Fastow's colleagues also benefited from business entities set up to make Enron's balance sheet look better by removing debt. Michael Kopper, one of Enron's financial managers, received millions of dollars as a result of establishing and managing such partnerships. Kopper and Fastow had ties outside the office, as well. The two lived in the same affluent Houston community; Kopper sold his previous home to Fastow's parents for $10—and Fastow became the guarantor of their $850,000 mortgage. Later, Kopper pleaded guilty for his role in money laundering and conspiracy to commit wire fraud at Enron and forfeited millions of dollars he gained from the Enron partnerships. "In order to effect the transactions," he told the court about his arrangement with Fastow, "I had to kick back money to the Enron CFO."[15]

Fastow sometimes vacationed with a high-ranking Merrill Lynch investment banker, Schuyler Tilney, whose wife was then a senior Enron manager. (Merrill Lynch later fired Tilney and another top executive after they refused to cooperate with federal investigators.) Apparently Merrill Lynch, eager to expand its investment banking relationship with Enron, pressured one of its analysts to boost ratings of Enron. That analyst left his job rather than do so, but another analyst went ahead with the higher ratings, which many investors consult before deciding to buy or sell a company's stock. Meanwhile, Merrill Lynch won more investment banking business from Enron and invested millions in one of the Enron partnerships led by Fastow.[16]

Conflicts of interest between a Wall Street firm's research analysts and its investment bankers can potentially hurt shareholders as well as employees. This is why New York's attorney general, securities regulators, and others are investigating potential conflicts at Merrill Lynch, Salomon Smith Barney, and other securities firms.[17] How can companies reduce the possibility that conflicts of interest will occur—and ensure that conflicts are completely and publicly disclosed if they do occur?

Legal Compliance

What happens when managers allow or even direct the destruction or removal of evidence that might link their firm to questionable activities? This was the situation faced by Arthur Andersen, the accounting firm that audited Enron's financial reports. After Enron's bankruptcy, government investigators began seeking information about Enron's audits. In response, Andersen's lawyers searched the accounting firm's computers and found that thousands of e-mails had been deleted. They also learned that cartons of documents had been shredded. Within months, a former Andersen partner admitted he had coordinated the shredding, agreed to plead guilty, and became a key witness in the government's case against Andersen for obstructing justice.[18]

The jury in that case focused on the questionable actions of one Andersen partner in the legal department. At the suggestion of this partner, Andersen's lead partner on the Enron account deleted potentially damaging wording from a document summarizing conversations between Andersen and Enron managers about Enron's financial results. The jury determined that this deletion was supposed to prevent the SEC from learning about misleading information that Enron would have included in an earnings report. As a result, the jury found Andersen guilty of obstructing justice, and the company began winding down its operations soon afterward.[19]

When a company or its board of directors detects fraud and cooperates with authorities to investigate, some managers may be indicted or agree to plead guilty to certain charges. However, if the company signs a corporate integrity agreement to settle the case, it will not be prosecuted as an organization (in contrast to the Andersen case, where the company itself was found guilty). The company will have to establish a legal compliance program under government supervision, appoint a compliance officer to keep the company on track, and agree to quickly report any questionable activity that comes to light. It will also have to fire every manager and employee involved in any crimes that are discovered. Such agreements often make headlines, although all the details are generally not disclosed.[20] How are stakeholders likely to react when they hear that a company they work for, have invested in, or buy from has signed a corporate integrity agreement?

Lawyers are important compliance advisors, helping managers understand their obligations and reviewing corporate plans and controls in light of applicable laws. Now lawyers are being enlisted in the fight against corporate wrong-doing. The Sarbanes-Oxley Act requires lawyers to report "evidence of a material violation of securities law or breach of fiduciary duty" to a company's general counsel (its top lawyer) as well as to the CEO and board of directors. This requirement was added because Senator Michael B. Enzi of Wyoming—who trained as an accountant—looked at the tangled financial webs woven by Enron and other bankrupt firms and realized that "probably in almost every transaction there was a lawyer who drew up the documents in that procedure." The senator reasoned that, in addition to enacting tougher standards for top managers and public accounting firms, "there ought to be some kind of an ethical standard put in place for the attorneys as well."[21]

Yet, as one securities lawyer points out, company lawyers are hired by management and work closely with executives and department managers every day. Having to report questionable tactics would put company lawyers in "a very, very difficult situation" and could mean they would be fired if they brought suspicious activities to the attention of the CEO and the board. Should company lawyers be forced to report potentially damaging information to their employers or be accountable to outside stakeholders?[22]

Insider Trading

Insider trading occurs when a manager or employee (a corporate insider) buys or sells stock based on significant information not available to the public. Legally, insiders (and some "outsiders" who are given inside information) are not allowed to buy or sell stock until such data becomes public knowledge. Ethically, insider trading violates the trust between a company's shareholders and its managers, who have a duty to safeguard the shareholders' financial interests.[23]

Insider trading is not new. It often made headlines in the 1980s, when Ivan Boesky paid $100 million to settle charges relating to trades he made as a result of inside information about corporate mergers and acquisitions. Although insider-trading cases declined during the first half of the 1990s—the SEC brought 29 cases of insider trading in 1996—by 2001 the number of cases had risen to 57. In 2002, the SEC approved new rules forcing companies to announce any buying or selling of shares by top management within two days, as a way to alert other stakeholders to insiders' trades.[24]

One of the highest-profile cases in recent years concerned CEO Samuel Waksal's sale of shares in ImClone Systems, a biotechnology firm. In 2002, Waksal was charged with trying to sell stock just ahead of an announcement that the Food and Drug Administration had not accepted the firm's application to sell a new cancer drug. In addition, the government alleged that Waksal warned family members and others to sell before the bad news became public and sent ImClone's share price tumbling. The government is also investigating whether Waksal destroyed evidence and made false statements to Congress as the case progressed.[25] Such cases, regardless of their outcomes, point up the serious ethical issues involved in how corporate insiders handle confidential information that can dramatically affect a stock's price once it is revealed.

CORPORATE GOVERNANCE

In public corporations, holders of common stock elect a board of directors who, in turn, are responsible for selecting and supervising the top executives who actually plan and manage day-to-day operations. The board is supposed to represent the interests of shareholders, in particular, while also considering the interests of employees, customers, and other stakeholders. Top management as well as board members often hold huge blocks of stock, so their interests should—in theory—be aligned with those of shareholders.

How, then, to account for the scope of the legal and ethical problems faced by Enron and other extremely troubled corporations? Congress has been probing just that question. "We are reviewing the extent and quality of management oversight by the boards of several of the companies new in crisis," legislators wrote to directors of Enron, Waste Management, Qwest, Global Crossing, Tyco, Adelphia, and seven other companies in mid-2002, adding: "A thorough examination of this matter is vital to restore confidence in American business and financial markets."[26]

No formal code of corporate governance exists in the United States, although Great Britain, Italy, and some other nations have adopted new rules affecting corporate control and management. These reforms were prompted, in part, by public revelations of controversial management decisions and financial deals that were either not detected or not halted by corporate boards. Although the specifics vary from country to country, the intent is the same: To make directors more accountable and more active in preventing corporate abuses that may harm stakeholders.[27]

Corporate governance has also been studied by a task force of the American Bar Association. "We have historically relied on the independence of key corporate leaders to keep their focus on the interests of shareholders," says ABA President Robert E. Hirshon. "The task force's core conclusion is that directors, auditors, and [legal] counsel have in too many instances fallen short of providing active, informed, and independent stewardship." One major issue addressed by the ABA task force is the composition of the board of directors, including whether directors are company officials, former company executives, or outsiders.[28]

Composition of the Board

Many corporations have both insiders and *independent directors* (also known as *outside directors*)—people not working for the company—serving on their boards. *Gray directors* are executives who work for suppliers or consultants that have significant business relationships with the company. Boards dominated by insiders (or loaded with gray directors) have more difficulty making objective decisions about company matters, including reviewing top management's performance and compensation. "Too many boards are composed of current and former CEOs who have a vested interest in maintaining a system that is beneficial to them," comments the chairman of Canada's Center for Corporate and Public Governance."[29] How can boards make unbiased decisions and act in stakeholders' best interests under such conditions?

When some or most of the directors hold huge blocks of stock, the overall board may be reluctant to take actions that could generate negative publicity and hurt the share price or embarrass the company. And corporate governance may suffer when a CEO personally selects directors, in effect creating a board that is more likely to rubber-stamp the CEO's proposals. Consider the situation at now-bankrupt Adelphia, a cable TV company. John Rigas and three other members of the founding Rigas family served as directors until Rigas and two of his sons were charged with misusing corporate funds in 2002. The SEC has also initiated a civil suit against the company, several Rigas family members, and other Adelphia business associates; and a federal grand jury has returned indictments charging Rigas, two of his sons, and two other executives with defrauding Adelphia's shareholders.[30]

Moreover, having the CEO chair the board sets up another potential conflict, because the chair cannot easily be objective about evaluating his or her own performance. CEOs chair the boards of most U.S. corporations. In contrast, to avoid potential conflicts and counter the power of the CEO, U.K. and Canadian corporations have independent directors chair their boards.[31]

Now more corporations are seeking independent directors to strengthen their boards. According to one survey, 92 percent of *Fortune 500* corporations want to create more independent boards that will question and probe corporate decisions and actions. At the same time, directors need to maintain cordial relations with each other and with management in order to get things done. This isn't always easy, says Esther Dyson, who sits on more than 12 boards:

"It's one of the hardest things in the world to sit in a board room and say, 'No, I don't think so' and cling to your point of view. Everybody thinks you're being disruptive and nitpicking."[32]

Some of the world's best-managed companies value independent directors because of their diverse experiences and views. General Electric's board, for example, headed by CEO Jeffrey Immelt, has a few insiders, such as the CEO of GE-owned NBC and the chairman of GE Capital Services. Most of its board consists of independent directors, including top executives of Sun Microsystems, Avon Products, Kimberly-Clark de Mexico, Ogilvy and Mather Worldwide, and other companies. In addition, one director is a Harvard Business School professor, one is a lawyer, and others are retired from senior management positions in business and banking.[33]

Role of the Audit Committee

Boards of directors establish committees to oversee specific corporate decisions and activities, including an audit committee to watch over the firm's financial affairs. The audit committee is expected to review reports from the accounting firm that audited the corporation's finances, look for proper internal controls, and check for unacceptable conflicts of interest. Ideally, these directors should be savvy (and independent) enough to grill management about murky transactions or cozy relations with auditors.

Yet at Riggs National Corp., the audit committee does not guarantee that the financial services firm's reports meet GAAP; Liz Claiborne and other companies also offer disclaimers about the limits of their audit committees' conclusions. Waste Management's financial statements specifically note that the audit committee relies only on information provided by management and auditors. "It is an explicit statement of what has always been the case," says the company's general counsel. "It doesn't change our audit committee's duties, responsibilities, or legal liabilities."[34] Even when directors have little or no hands-on experience with accounting or financial reporting, what ethical responsibilities do those serving on audit committees owe to shareholders and other stakeholders?

Enron's audit committee was chaired by an independent director, a former Stanford University accounting professor, for more than 10 years. Yet according to Senate investigators looking into Enron's corporate governance in the wake of its bankruptcy, the committee did not object when Arthur Andersen auditors reported that the company's accounting practices were "high risk," "pushing limits," and "at the edge" of GAAP. Such briefings occurred in 1999, 2000, and 2001, but committee members apparently did not push for more details or suggest taking a more conservative approach. Lawyers for the independent directors say that management misled the committee. On the other hand, a report prepared later, by an Enron director who reviewed the board's overall performance, noted that its committees reviewed information "only in a cursory way" and said the board did not understand "the significance of some of the specific information that came before it." A *Business Week* article called this "as complete a definition of 'asleep at the wheel' as you'll ever find."[35] See the section on accounting practices, later in this chapter, for more about how audit committees can probe for auditing problems.

Role of Stakeholders

As stakeholders, legislators and regulators clearly hold considerable power when investigating corporate governance problems and shaping new policies and practices. Individual shareholders, except for a few outside investors with large stakes in a company, rarely have anywhere near the clout needed to influence board decisions or committees. Shareholders can attend a company's annual meeting and vote on such questions as electing directors, changing auditors, and other issues at hand. Those who cannot attend are entitled to vote by submitting a *proxy*—written, oral, or electronic authorization to have another party vote shares on their behalf for or against each question—in advance of the annual meeting. Yet fewer than three-quarters of all shareholders bother to vote by proxy, and small shareholders are the least likely to do so. As a result, proposals backed by management usually pass with minimal resistance.[36]

On the other hand, pension funds and investment funds that own thousands or even millions of shares in a company can be extremely effective in pushing for corporate governance reform. The California Public Employees Retirement System (CalPERS), one of the country's largest pension funds, has publicly campaigned and even sued, in some cases, to force corporations to adopt certain reforms and be held more accountable. CalPERS is one of the pension funds suing WorldCom and its former top officials as well as several major banks over losses stemming from the funds' purchases of WorldCom bonds.[37] To end conflicts of interest, it also requires the investment banking firms with which it does business to sever any internal ties linking the firms' research analysts with their investment banking personnel.[38]

Moreover, labor unions, which have more than $3 trillion in pension-fund holdings, are advocating governance reforms. In 2001, the United Association of Plumbers and three unions—which together hold $93 million worth of the company's stock—wanted Walt Disney to stop hiring its accounting firm for consulting work, citing potential conflicts of interest. Disney resisted but the SEC forced the company to put the unions' proposal on the ballot for voting at the annual shareholders' meeting in early 2002. As the meeting neared, however, scandals at Enron and other companies prompted Disney to announce it would no longer buy consulting services from its auditor. "We didn't need someone to tell us that our shareholders would expect this of us," said Disney's CFO. Strong shareholder support for this decision encouraged Disney to enact even more stringent checks on auditor services.[39]

As another example, Lawndale Capital Management invests $5 million to $10 million in smaller public companies so it can push for better corporate governance measures, such as a predominance of independent directors and allowing board votes only when half or more of the directors present are independent. If suggestions to the board and top management are not accepted, the fund goes to the press, lines up other investors to support the ideas, and even proposes qualified people to serve as independent directors. Other funds are following Lawndale's lead to promote governance change at more companies. "The bottom line is that good governance enhances operating performance," says Andy Shapiro, the fund's founder.[40]

Insurance firms are also stakeholders, in that corporate governance actions can affect their performance. Why? Because insurers provide companies with directors and officers liability insurance to cover any payouts from investor lawsuits over questionable accounting and other practices. Against a backdrop of multi-million dollar bankruptcies and a flurry of lawsuits alleging fraud and other problems, some insurers are refusing to cover companies with inferior internal controls and other problems. Others are forcing companies to open their financial records and audit reports, strengthen their boards, and tighten director oversight of management practices. As a result of insurers' involvement, companies are paying higher premiums, putting their boards and controls under closer scrutiny, and—in some cases—having difficulty recruiting independent directors.[41] What are the implications for more ethical corporate governance?

ACCOUNTING PRACTICES

The bankruptcies of Enron and WorldCom, among other major scandals, have their roots in the way these firms accounted for business transactions and reported their financial condition. The chief financial officer has overall responsibility for planning and managing the company's day-to-day and long-term finances. The controller is responsible for the firm's accounting and financial reporting activities as well as for audits to ensure reporting accuracy and compliance with legal and regulatory guidelines. The treasurer decides how to invest any excess cash and manage funds so the company can meet its financial obligations. Together, these three managers and their staff members are to help the company move toward its profit goals while providing appropriate data to government regulators, owners and shareholders, employees, and other stakeholders by following GAAP. They face a variety of ethical (and legal) challenges, however.

Following GAAP

GAAP falls under the Financial Accounting Standards Board (FASB), made up of academic members, experienced corporate accounting experts, and accountants from major CPA firms. The SEC gives FASB the power it needs to establish the GAAP rules that public corporations must follow. The SEC has created a new Public Company Accounting Oversight Board, with a five-member board composed of CPAs and non-accountants, to oversee accounting issues related to the financial reporting of U.S. public corporations.[42]

The European Union is also tightening its rules for closer scrutiny of corporate accounting and auditing under the International Accounting Standards Board. The accounting rules set by the United Kingdom's Accounting Standards Board force auditors to stick to the spirit as well as the letter of the law. In contrast, U.S. auditors may follow GAAP and still report figures that give an incomplete or misleading picture of a company's true financial situation.[43] Is this ethical?

Under GAAP, company managers have considerable latitude in the financial assumptions and accounting decisions they make. A former SEC chairman called this "the gray area between legitimacy and outright fraud." GAAP requires companies to depreciate the cost of a piece of equipment over its useful life, for example, but allows companies to decide what lifetime estimates to use—and to change depreciation schedules when they believe they have more accurate estimates. An airline's decision to spread the cost of a multimillion dollar jet over a longer schedule means lower expenses during each year, leading to higher net income during those years. This is only one of the ways companies manage their financial reporting through special handling of expenses and revenues.[44]

Handling Expenses and Revenues

Companies use a variety of accounting techniques that are allowed under GAAP but may obscure actual financial results. For example:[45]

- *Boosting profits through one-time transactions.* When sales do not provide the profit boost that management is seeking, a company may sell its own stock or use another one-time transaction to show a gain and improve the figures. Analysts generally look more closely at the underlying figures from ongoing operations when they spot nonrecurring transactions.

- *Reducing current expenses through a depreciation change.* AMR (the parent of American Airlines) reduced its depreciation expense by $158 million in 2000 by lengthening the depreciation schedule on some of its jets to 25 years. As a result,

AMR reported lower depreciation expenses, which in turn improved net earnings by $99 million—slightly more than 10 percent of the overall earnings reported that year. Analysts look at this kind of change when evaluating the "quality" of a company's earnings increase; "high quality" earnings come from selling more goods and services, selling products at higher prices, or slashing ongoing expenses.

Companies sometimes use the following shady accounting techniques to boost current revenue, raising serious ethical questions:

- *Prematurely recording revenue.* Sunbeam boosted revenue by "pre-selling" gas grills to retailers one fall, booking the sales as income, allowing retailers to pay six months later, and warehousing the grills for shipment in the spring. Sunbeam did not expect to ship the goods or receive payment for months but still labeled these transactions as current sales so it could report higher revenue at the end of its fiscal year. This clearly violated GAAP.

- *Fabricating revenue.* To inflate revenue, some companies have actually resorted to recording nonexistent sales transactions. In fact, nearly 20 percent of the earnings misstatements that occurred from 1995 to 1999 involved entirely fictitious transactions—again, clear violations of GAAP.

- *Improperly reporting liabilities.* Enron made its financials look better than they actually were by failing to disclose certain liabilities that would have lowered profits. Not making the proper disclosures and making misleading disclosures violate GAAP.

As noted earlier, WorldCom managers used a different and unacceptable approach to make the firm's earnings look better by minimizing the impact of billions of dollars in expenses. Instead of recording these costs as operating expenses and deducting them from current income, the company called them capital expenses and spread them over a number of years. This had the effect of reducing charges against current income, thereby improving reported profits. However, after disclosing these and other accounting irregularities, WorldCom restated its finances for 1999 through 2001 to show much lower profits.[46]

Other companies have also announced restatements and accounting changes in recent years. Even as the SEC was investigating its accounting practices in 2002, debt-ridden Qwest Communications International implemented an accounting change. Before, the telecommunications firm accounted for its yellow pages sales and expenses when each directory was published. With the change, Qwest decided to spread sales and expenses throughout the life of each directory, a move that reduced its 2001 directory sales revenue by $80 million.[47]

The SEC is looking more closely at a variety of questionable accounting practices, such as: reporting merchandise on consignment as sales; booking revenue on purchases that customers are not required to pay for; boosting sales by weakening credit standards without allowing for more bad debts or returns; booking rebates from suppliers as revenue when these funds are linked to future required purchases; and booking the proceeds from a loan or an investment as revenue.[48] Is it ethical for a company to mask problems or make results look rosier through accounting?

Taking A New Look at Old Practices

With the bankruptcy of Enron and other giants, analysts, regulators, auditors, and investors are taking a new look at some accounting practices that were used in the past. In the energy and telecommunications industries, among others, companies have been known to boost revenue through *round-trip transactions.* In such a transaction, company A sells certain energy or capacity to company B while company B sells slightly different energy or capacity to company A. Yet the firms may use entirely different methods to account for these sales, as when Global Crossing and Qwest Communications sold each other $200 million worth of fiber-optic network telecommunications capacity. Although Global Crossing (now bankrupt) and Qwest say their accounting followed GAAP, the SEC has been inspecting their records to determine if the roundtrip transactions had an actual business purpose. Otherwise, the transactions could be "materially misleading" and could be considered fraudulent. Allegations that Enron used round-trip transactions to increase its revenue are also prompting a new look at this practice.[49]

Another common practice getting a fresh look is the use of "pro forma" accounting. From the Latin for "for form," this term refers to figures that management presents by eliminating selected costs. One pro forma presentation used since the 1970s is abbreviated EBITDA—earnings before interest, taxes, depreciation, and amortization. Clearly, deducting interest, taxes, and other costs will make earnings look smaller. For instance, the cable television firm Charter Communications reported EBITDA of $1.8 billion in 2001; deducting capital expenses, however, transforms the financial picture into a loss of $1.2 billion. For their part, managers who use EBITDA say it helps analysts and investors better gauge results from a company's core operations, especially in cable television and other industries requiring costly capital investments.[50] This debate is bringing the ethics of pro forma accounting to the attention of more investors.

Also being examined in a new light: How companies use special-purpose entities, limited partnerships, and other methods of keeping certain figures off their balance sheets. Legitimate special-purpose entities are used to finance research-and-development ventures and other business activities that need not be reported on the balance sheet. However, Enron and other companies apparently used special-purpose entities as a way to boost earnings. Enron set up as many as 850 special-purpose entities; one, called Chewco, improved its parent's income by $600 million. Enron also used limited partnerships to blur the extent of its debt position. By one estimate, these partnerships hid at least $700 million in debt that should have appeared on Enron's books.[51]

Now that regulators, analysts, and investors are digging deeper into corporate figures, a growing number of firms are expanding their mandated financial reports and beefing up disclosure of all sorts of transactions and activities. "Companies are increasing disclosure not because they are necessarily altruistic or scared they are going to be put in jail, but because the market is demanding it now," comments a stock research expert. General Electric added more pages to its glossy 2001 annual report to shareholders, issued in 2002, to allow for expanded explanations of its special-purpose entities. Xerox published a 1,000-page document in 2002 to explain its restatement of five years' worth of revenue following a settlement with the SEC (and payment of a $10 million fine). More detail is not necessarily better detail—nor is a heftier document any easier for investors to comprehend—but legal and regulatory trends are nudging corporations in the direction of more information released more quickly.[52]

Working with Auditors

Where were the auditors when Enron, WorldCom, and other companies were fiddling with their finances? KPMG and other CPA firms are hired to study the books of their corporate clients, sample transactions to check for proper bookkeeping, examine controls on fraud and other potential problems, and then report whether the accounting follows GAAP. Yet accounting professors Steve Sutton of the University of Connecticut and Charles Cullinan of Bryant College say auditors today look more at internal controls than at specific accounts on a company's books—which reduces the likelihood of catching fraud on a major scale, especially when top management is involved. In fact, when studying SEC enforcement actions, the professors found that the CEO was involved in more than two-thirds of the 276 frauds that occurred between 1987 and 1999. To detect fraud, the professors say corporations will need to have auditors delve well below the surface of transactions, which would require more time and cost companies more in audit fees.[53]

The chairman of the Public Oversight Board, a self-regulation group for accountants, agrees that the scandals in which auditors failed to find fraud were due to the more difficult nature of the auditing needed to examine today's complex financial transactions. The American Institute of Certified Public Accountants, an industry organization, stresses that CPAs annually check the accounting of more than 15,000 public corporations and are accused of mistakes in only .1 % (or about 15) of the audits. At the same time, a former SEC chief accountant points out that investors lost more than $100 billion due to fraud and earnings restatements from 1995 to 2001. Responding to the rising tide of frauds and scandals, accountants say that self-regulation through the Public Oversight Board is the way to strengthen reporting and auditing rules. Yet this regulatory board lacks the power to enforce compliance and discipline auditors who violate the rules. Moreover, since the board was established in 1977, it has never announced a negative review of a major CPA firm.[54]

Scandals such as the Enron bankruptcy have brought to the forefront the ethical issue of whether CPA firms are caught in a conflict of interest when they provide both auditing and consulting services to corporate clients. In addition, corporate executives are dealing with the issue of how to check on the auditors they hire to check on their financial reports.

Auditing and Consulting

How tough and objective can a CPA firm be when it receives more in consulting fees than it receives in auditing fees from the same corporate client? This question is being asked about Arthur Andersen's relationship with Enron. In 2000, as one example, Enron paid Andersen $25 million for auditing and $27 million for consulting. That year, after Andersen's consulting group broke away from the auditing group to do business as Accenture, the auditing group began rebuilding its consulting business and pushing for revenue growth. By early 2001, Andersen partners were privately discussing Enron's accounting techniques and whether to remain its auditor. Internal e-mails show that Andersen's top accounting experts did not always agree with Enron's accounting decisions; in at least four instances, the Andersen audit team took Enron's side but did not notify Andersen's top accounting experts, a violation of internal policies. By December, 2001, Enron had declared bankruptcy and Andersen was defending its auditing efforts.[55]

Concerned about even the appearance of a conflict of interest that might spring from hiring a CPA firm for both auditing and consulting—and under shareholder pressure—Walt Disney and other companies are halting the practice. Shareholders are pushing other corporations to follow suit, and top managers at other companies are proactively curtailing the consulting services they receive from their CPA firms. Regulators may mandate such a separation of services in the future to avoid potential conflicts.[56]

Checks on Auditors

As discussed earlier, the audit committee of the board of directors is responsible for supervising the work of the CPA firm that examines the company's financial records. The role of the audit committee, according to Berkshire Hathaway chairman Warren Buffet, "is to hold the auditor's feet to the fire" by asking probing questions and including the answers in the committee's official records of its meetings.

He suggests that the audit committee ask the CPA firm questions such as:[57]

- "If the auditor were solely responsible for preparation of the company's financial statements, would they have been prepared in any way differently than the manner selected by management?"

- "Is the auditor aware of any operational or accounting activities that had the effect of moving revenues or expenses between quarters?"

The goal is to spark more interaction between members of the audit committee and the auditors and to uncover and address potential problems so the corporation's financial reports are more accurate and substantive. This dialogue also puts the CPA firm on notice that the company expects it to use high standards when auditing the books.[58] Other suggested reforms are to have audit committees meet more frequently and for longer periods to better understand the complexities of the corporation's finances and the auditors' work; increase pay for directors who serve on audit committees as compensation for a heavier workload; recruit more financially-savvy directors for audit committees; allow the audit committee to hire the CPA firm and talk with auditors (without company managers present) about any accounting issues; and require companies to switch auditing firms every few years.[59]

With closer SEC scrutiny of corporate finances expected after so many major bankruptcies, more companies are hiring CPAs to conduct "mock SEC inspections." These inspections check on internal compliance levels and uncover possible problems for management to investigate more closely. Although mock inspections may cost more than $25,000, the price is small compared to the public embarrassment a company could suffer if the SEC finds problems and the corporation's name is splashed over the front page of the *Wall Street Journal*.[60]

ETHICAL DECISIONS AND BEHAVIOR

Despite the recent rash of corporate scandals, most companies believe in—and adhere to—appropriate ethical standards. Since the 1930s, Johnson & Johnson (J&J) has followed a written company credo that names customers as the top responsibility. In order of priority after customers, it says it is responsible to its 100,000 employees, the communities in which it operates, and its shareholders. J&J made headlines for acting ethically in 1982, when it recalled all Tylenol products from store shelves after reports of seven deaths linked to bottles that had been tampered with. This recall cost $100 million but management, guided by the company credo, believed the action was ethically necessary to protect customers. Over the years, the Tylenol episode has become a case study in applying strict ethical standards, and it has raised public expectations of J&J's ethical behavior. "More is expected of us than other companies," acknowledges J&J's CEO. "That's totally fair."[61]

J&J is not alone in its commitment to ethical behavior. Procter & Gamble's stand on ethics dates back 140 years to the Civil War era. During that war, many companies saw an opportunity to boost profits by selling inferior products at inflated prices to the military.

However, P&G's management refused to follow suit and, unlike many companies, provided good-quality products such as candles and soap to fulfill its military contracts.[62]

Does promoting ethical decisions and behavior within the organization pay off? In the long run, the answer is a resounding 'yes.' P&G, J&J, and other ethical companies are still in business, whereas Enron and other companies led by managers who made dubious decisions are in bankruptcy. Still, companies cannot expect a tangible payback in the short term. "If ethical behavior paid, everyone would always be ethical," says Professor Richard Tedlow of Harvard Business School. "The difficulty with trust and character is that it doesn't show up on a balance sheet."[63]

Legislative, regulatory, and court actions have added powerful incentives for U.S. firms to promote ethical actions. The Foreign Corrupt Practices Act, in force for nearly 25 years, forbids U.S. firms operating in other countries from paying bribes and taking other steps considered unethical in the United States. Under this law, however, firms may offer small payments to foreign officials for expediting routine transactions. Some U.S. companies complain that the law hampers their ability to compete with non-U.S. firms that use bribes and other outlawed methods to win business. Yet others refer to the law when explaining why they cannot do something that is legal or customary in another country. Ethics programs are also important because, under 1991 legislation, U.S. companies found guilty of business crimes may be treated less harshly if they have programs in place to uncover dubious activities. Corporate directors, in particular, may be interested in promoting ethics programs since a Delaware court ruled in 1996 that directors of companies lacking adequate compliance plans to prevent illegalities may be held personally liable.[64]

Among the techniques companies use to instill and support ethical behavior throughout the organization are codes of conduct, ethics training, and accommodation of whistleblowers. But writing a memo about an ethics code or requiring all employees to attend ethics training is not enough. Research shows that ethics codes and programs are more effective when they are woven into the cultural fiber of the firm through top-management leadership and the consistent use of appropriate sanctions and rewards to reinforce accountability. "No code ever works unless its operation is embedded in a culture and accepted by those in the culture," observes Professor Alasdair MacIntyre of the University of Notre Dame.[65]

Codes of Conduct

A *code of conduct* (or *ethics code*) is a written statement of the principles and policies that a company's managers and employees are expected to apply on the job. In addition to discussing ethical issues, many cover legal issues such as bribery, theft, discrimination, and sexual harassment. In one study, 60 percent of the corporate codes examined mentioned relations between management and employees; 60 percent mentioned environmental issues; 48 percent mentioned consumer protection; and 23 percent mentioned bribery (of employees as well as by employees).[66] In addition, companies may want to augment organization-wide codes with a few particulars for each division or unit. "Keep it clear and concise, and avoid 'legalese' and loopholes," one legal expert advises.[67]

Nearly every large U.S. corporation has a code of ethics to guide the conduct of managers and employees. Public companies whose stock is traded on the New York Stock Exchange must have a written code of conduct for their work force as well as their directors. Codes of conduct are also commonly established by corporations in the United Kingdom and throughout Europe.[68]

In addition, many professional and industry organizations have also established codes of conduct. To illustrate, the Pharmaceutical Research and Manufacturers of America has a voluntary code of conduct that discourages drug companies from offering gifts that do not primarily benefit patients. Under this code, drug companies could ethically provide doctors with anatomical models for their offices but not give doctors blocks of tickets to sporting events. Some states are backing up such voluntary industry codes with legal authority. In Vermont, drug companies are required to report any gifts to doctors that exceed $25 in value.[69]

Having a code is only the first step. Companies must then integrate it into everyday activities at every level. Professor Lynn Sharp Paine suggests "building adherence to standards into management systems, into performance evaluation, compensation, audit, and control." The code of ethics at Enron, for instance, stated that "business is to be conducted in compliance . . . with the highest professional and ethical standards." All new employees had to sign a statement of ethics when hired, and the board's audit committee was to oversee compliance with legal and ethical policies. Yet "at Enron, ethics was simply a piece of paper with three Ps—print, post, and then pray that something is actually going to happen," says the president of the Ethics Resource Center.[70]

Underscoring its commitment to ethical behavior, Dow Chemical recently asked every employee in its financial department to sign a new, stricter code of conduct. The company has a long tradition of upholding its code of conduct despite global differences in attitudes and behavior. When Dow's CFO headed the company's Italian operations some years ago, he turned down deals that entailed actions running counter to the company's code of conduct. "But when scandals came up with government officials in Italy," the CFO recalls, "Dow's name never got mentioned." In addition, Dow recently launched a five-year program of intensive training to help its worldwide workers handle ethical and legal issues, one example of today's trend toward increased use of ethics training.[71]

Ethics Training

To highlight the nature and importance of ethical decisions and behavior, many companies offer ethics training to managers and employees alike. Sometimes the training is provided during orientation for newly-hired employees; sometimes it is offered as part of an ongoing developmental training program; and sometimes it is provided to all employees as a periodic reinforcement of ethical principles. Dow, for example, is customizing its ethics training based on specific job functions. Managers and employees who negotiate contracts might receive more training in antitrust and bribery concerns; supervisors might receive more training in handling workplace harassment. Dow's Global Law Officers are also contacting all departments to ensure they have all the resources they need for legal compliance.[72]

Not every company offers ethics training, nor does every company back it up with director involvement. One recent study of 136 large U.S. corporations found that just over half had no ethics program; 25 percent had an ethics program coupled with active oversight by the board of directors; and 17 percent had an ethics program without active board oversight. Interestingly, few insurance and media companies in the study had an ethics program, whereas more than half of the food, beverage, and tobacco firms had a program.[73]

Defense contractors are among the most proactive in providing ethics training. An industry group reports on best-practices guidelines and training ideas to help managers and employees recognize and properly address ethical challenges. Defense contractor Lockheed Martin posts its extensive ethics code on the company Web site (www.lockheedmartin.com) and backs it up with ethics leadership training tailored for managers at different levels, starting at the top. (See the listing of ethics resources online, at the end of this chapter, for links to other corporate ethics codes.) Lockheed's employees receive training from interactive CD-ROMs, Web-based quizzes, classroom programs, and other methods. Ethical guidelines are translated into different languages for every nation where Lockheed operates. The company recently established a "Chairman's Award for Ethical Conduct" to honor adherence to high ethical standards. It also maintains a cadre of 65 ethics officers to support compliance and helps suppliers create ethics training programs. And its management takes action when warranted. During one recent year, Lockheed fired 52 employees for unethical actions.[74]

Whistleblowers

A *whistleblower* is an employee or manager who calls attention to a company's unethical or illegal practices. Accountant Sherron Watkins is the whistleblower who sent a memo alerting Enron's CEO to concerns about the company's convoluted financial dealings. In part, her memo read, "I realize that we have a lot of smart people looking at this and a lot of accountants including AA&Co [Arthur Andersen] have blessed the accounting treatment. None of that will protect Enron if these transactions are ever disclosed in the bright light of day." Stuart Zisman, one of Enron's corporate lawyers, also warned his managers that the firm's finances were "cooked in order to eliminate the drag on earnings." Zisman's manager reacted by criticizing the harsh language of the whistleblower's warning. As later events showed, the serious concerns raised by Zisman and Watkins—and other Enron personnel—were quite valid.[75]

Cynthia Cooper, an internal auditor for WorldCom, is another recent whistleblower. Investigating the accounting treatment of some capital expenses, she failed to get an adequate explanation from the company's CFO and controller, so she called the questionable transactions to the attention of the director heading WorldCom's audit committee. This started the firm toward the revelations about improper accounting that ultimately helped push it into bankruptcy.[76]

Whistleblowers sometimes face fierce resistance and resentment inside the organization when they try to expose suspect actions. Retaliation is illegal, but companies and government agencies sometimes attempt to discredit whistleblowers, transfer them to undesirable duties or shifts, or take other steps in response to allegations. For example, when Roy Olofson was vice president of finance for the telecommunications firm Global Crossing, he wrote to the company's head lawyer about dubious accounting practices. Months later, Global Crossing filed for bankruptcy and Congress began investigating its financial situation. By then, Olofson had left the company; he later filed suit over being forced out.[77]

Under the intense pressure, whistleblowers sometimes lose their nerve, their family and friends, their professional standing, and even their health. Experts advise employees to talk with family members and legal counsel before speaking out, carefully document any actions they believe are suspect, learn how the company treated any previous whistleblowers, bring their concerns to the proper internal authorities, and allow the organization time to respond before talking with members of the media or other outsiders about the allegations.[78]

Most firms are very interested in halting illegal and unethical practices by accommodating whistleblowers. Dow Chemical, for example, maintains an ethics hotline for employees to report questionable decisions and behavior, supported by an ethics compliance committee to review and investigate allegations. Outsiders monitor the committee's actions to ensure that whistleblowers' complaints are thoroughly and fairly examined.[79] Lockheed Martin asks employees to report suspected legal and ethical violations using confidential, toll-free hotlines or a confidential post office box. Employees can also contact people in the company's ethics office by fax, e-mail, or in person.[80] Employees in these firms—and in the many other companies with well-developed ethics programs—receive a clear message that management is quite serious about business ethics, even in uncertain times.

CRITICAL THINKING EXERCISES

For Review

1. How is corporate culture likely to affect ethical decision-making and behavior within an organization?

2. What is a conflict of interest? Identify two conflicts of interest faced by some of the firms discussed in this chapter.

3. What is the Sarbanes-Oxley Act and how does it affect management accountability?

4. Why should corporate boards be dominated by independent directors?

5. How is the audit committee of a corporation's board of directors expected to safeguard the interests of shareholders?

6. How can shareholders encourage ethical decisions and behavior among managers of public companies?

7. What are some questionable accounting practices companies have used to disguise financial problems or improve reported earnings?

8. What issues are raised by a corporation's use of one accounting firm for both auditing and consulting services?

9. How can management instill and support ethical behavior throughout a company?

For Discussion and Analysis

1. Johnson & Johnson's company credo, designed to guide managers in making ethical decisions, states that the firm's top responsibility is to customers. Should all businesses make customers their first priority when balancing stakeholders' interests? Outline the arguments

for and against this position, drawing on material in this supplement, as well as your perspective as a customer, to illustrate your points.

2. Just as stakeholders have a right to expect ethical behavior from a company, a company should be able to expect ethical behavior from its stakeholders. Select one stakeholder group (such as customers or suppliers) and identify at least three ethical issues that this group might face in connection with a particular company. Why are these issues important for the stakeholder group and the company? What might a company do to encourage ethical behavior and decisions among members of this stakeholder group?

For Further Research

Working individually or in a team (as your instructor directs), use this chapter's listing of online ethics resources to locate codes of conduct from two companies and one professional association. What types of activities and situations are addressed by each code? How are the three codes similar and how are they different? How do these codes help managers and employees make ethical decisions about conflicts that may arise from trying to satisfy the needs and interests of various stakeholder groups? Select one code of conduct and suggest at least two improvements to address specific ethical challenges examined in this supplement.

ETHICS RESOURCES ONLINE

Check these Web sites for more information about ethical issues and assessments, codes of conduct, and other information related to contemporary business ethics.

www.business.com/directory/management/business_ethics/

This Business.com directory features links to numerous ethics sites, articles about ethical considerations, and other resources.

www.ethics.ubc.ca/resources/business/codes.html

The Center for Applied Ethics Web site offers convenient links to many organizations' codes of ethical conduct.

www.ethicsandbusiness.org/toolbox.htm

At the Center for Ethics and Business Web site, visitors can complete a self-assessment of ethical style and read about strategies for resolving ethical dilemmas.

www.iit.edu/departments/csep/PublicWWW/codes/business.html

The Center for the Study of Ethics in the Professions at Illinois Institute of Technology offers links to the codes of ethics posted by various professional groups.

www.thecorporatelibrary.com

Research general information about corporate ethics at the Corporate Library/International

Corporate Governance Research Web site.

www-1.ibm.com/partnerworld/pwhome.nsf/weblook/guide_index.html

This Web site presents IBM's detailed code of ethical conduct.

www.jpl.nasa.gov/JPL/ethics/

The Jet Propulsion Laboratory's Ethics Program is presented here.

www.lockheedmartin.com

Defense contractor Lockheed Martin posts its ethics code on the company's Web site.

http://ethics.wharton.upenn.edu

This Web site, from the Wharton School of the University of Pennsylvania, links to articles

about key ethical issues as well as to the school's ethics curriculum and other resources.

www.bsr.org/

Business for Social Responsibility is an organization devoted to promoting business ethics. Its

Web site offers analyses, news links, and other information.

www.crossroadsprograms.com/corporate.html

This Web site presents Crossroads Consulting's 25-question Corporate Integrity Checklist.

REFERENCES

_____

1. John R. Boatright, *Ethics and the Conduct of Business, 4th ed.* (Upper Saddle River, N.J.: Prentice Hall, 2003), pp. 21-22.

2. "Too Creative By 50%?" *The Economist,* July 6, 2002, pp. 57-58.

3. Stephen Labaton, "Will Reforms with Few Teeth Be Able to Bite?" *New York Times,* September 22, 2002, sec. 3, p. 4; Paula Dwyer, "Making Them Give Back the Cash," *Business Week,* August 26, 2002, p. 36; Jerry Markon and Jared Sandberg, "Two Ex-WorldCom Officials Charged with Securities Fraud," *Wall Street Journal,* July 16, 2002, www.wsj.com; Howard Fineman and Michael Isikoff, "Laying Down the Law," *Newsweek,* August 5, 2002, pp. 20-25; Herb Greenberg, "Legal—But Lousy," *Fortune,* September 2, 2002, p. 192.

4. Jonathan D. Glater, "Five Questions for Mary Jo White: Those Very Public Arrests of Executives," *New York Times,* July 28, 2002, sec. 3, p. 4; Fineman and Isikoff, "Laying Down the Law."

5. Gary Strauss, "How Did Business Get So Darn Dirty?" *USA Today,* June 12, 2002, www.usatoday.com; Fineman and Isikoff, "Laying Down the Law;" "When Something Is Rotten: Corporate Culture," *The Economist,* July 27, 2002, pp. 53-54.

6. William J. Holstein, "Fallout From a Free-for-All," *New York Times,* July 28, 2002, sec. 3, p. 6.

7. Heesun Wee, "Corporate Ethics: Right Makes Might," *Business Week Online,* April 11, 2002, www.businessweek.com.

8. Diana B. Henriques, "Those Old-Time Shares Are Looking Good Again," *New York Times,* August 18, 2002, sec. 4, p. 6.

9. "When Something Is Rotten: Corporate Culture."

10. "Why Honesty is the Best Policy," *The Economist,* March 9, 2002, pp. 9-13; "When Something Is Rotten: Corporate Culture."

11. Monica Roman, "True Confessions from CFOs," *Business Week,* August 12, 2002, p. 40.

12. "Why Honesty is the Best Policy."

13. George Anders, "Honesty Is the Best Policy—Trust Us," *Fast Company,* August 2000, pp. 262+.

14. Boatright, *Ethics and the Conduct of Business,* pp. 138-140; "Merrill Has to Face the Music," *Business Week,* August 12, 2002, p. 116.

15. Jonathan Weil and Kathryn Kranhold, "Ex-Enron Executive Kopper Will Plead Guilty to Fraud," *Wall Street Journal,* August 21, 2002, pp. 1+; Jonathan Weil, Alexei Barrionuevo, and Kathryn Kranhold, "A Guilty Plea by Enron's Kopper," *Wall Street Journal,* August 22, 2002, pp. 1+; "The Charge Sheet," *The Economist,* September 14, 2002, p. 62.

16. "At Merrill, They're History," *Business Week,* September 30, 2002, p. 48; "Merrill Has to Face the Music;" Paula Dwyer and Laura Cohn, "Merrill Lynch: See No Evil?" *Business Week,* September 16, 2002, pp. 68-76.

17. Gretchen Morgenson, "In a Broker's Notes, Trouble for Salomon," *New York Times,* September 22, 2002, sec. 3, pp. 1, 13; Mark Gimein, "Eliot Spitzer the Enforcer," *Fortune,* September 16, 2002, pp. 76+; Charles Gasparino, "NASD Plans to File Charges Against Salomon, Grubman," *Wall Street Journal*, September 20, 2002, pp. 1+.

18. Kurt Eichenwald, "Miscues, Missteps and the Fall of Andersen," *New York Times,* May 8, 2002, pp. C1+.

19. Kurt Eichenwald, "Andersen Guilty in Effort to Block Inquiry on Enron," *New York Times,* June 16, 2002, pp. 1+.

20. Joan Elise Dubinsky, "Speaking of Ethics: When Internal Audit Is the Last to Know About a CIA," *Preventing Business Fraud,* February 2002, p. 1.

21. Jonathan D. Glater, "Round Up the Usual Suspects. Lawyers, Too?" *New York Times,* August 4, 2002, sec. 3, p. 4.

22. Glater, "Round Up the Usual Suspects."

23. Boatright, *Ethics and the Conduct of Business,* pp. 350-353.

24. Debora Vrana and Walter Hamilton, "ImClone Inquiry: Insider Trading an Issue That Won't Go Away," *Los Angeles Times,* June 13, 2002, p. C1.

25. Chris Adams, "House Panel Turns Up the Heat On Waksal in ImClone Probe," *The Wall Street Journal,* August 20, 2002, www.wsj.com; Andrew Pollack, "Federal Judge Grants More Time in ImClone Insider Case," *New York Times,* July 27, 2002, p. 2; "The Charge Sheet."

26. Julie Mason, "Congress to Look at 13 Corporations; Directors Must Account for Oversight," *Houston Chronicle,* July 9, 2002, www.houstonchronicle.com.

27. John Rossant, "The Corporate Cleanup Goes Global," *Business Week,* May 6, 2002, pp. 80-81.

28. "ABA Corporate Responsibility Task Force Recommends New Corporate Governance Standards, Lawyer Ethics Rules," American Bar Association news release, July 24, 2002, www.abanet.org/media.

29. John A. Byrne, "How to Fix Corporate Governance," *Business Week,* May 6, 2002, pp. 68-78; Andrew J. Felo, "Ethics Programs, Board Involvement, and Potential Conflicts of Interest in Corporate Governance," *Journal of Business Ethics* 32 (2001): pp. 205-218.

30. Jerry Markon, "Federal Grand Jury Indicts Former Adelphia Officials," *Wall Street Journal,* September 24, 2002, www.wsj.com; "Corporate Governance: Designed by Committee," *The Economist,* June 15, 2002, pp. 69-71; "The Charge Sheet."

31. Joe Cappo, "Clearing the Air of Foul Corporate Practices," *Crain's Chicago Business,* July 15, 2002, p. 8; "Corporate Governance: Designed by Committee;" Byrne, "How to Fix Corporate Governance."

32. Susan Stellin, "Directors Ponder New, Tougher Roles," *New York Times,* June 30, 2002, sec. 3, p. 16.

33. General Electric annual report 2001.

34. Emily Thornton, "Audit Committees' New Duck-and-Cover," *Business Week,* April 15, 2002, p. 106.

35. Byrne, "How to Fix Corporate Governance;" Byrne, "No Excuses for Enron's Board," *Business Week,* July 29, 2002, pp. 50+.

36. Gretchen Morgenson, "Pick Up the Proxy, Fill It Out and Exert Some Control," *New York Times,* August 23, 2002, sec. 3, p. 1.

37. Paul Beckett and Jathon Sapsford, "California Pension Funds' Lawsuit Alleges Bond Fraud by WorldCom," *Wall Street Journal*, July 17, 2002, www.wsj.com.

38. Jeff Sommer, "Calpers Adopts Policy on Analyst Conflicts," *New York Times,* August 25, 2002, sec. 3, p. 7.

39. Amy Borrus, "Getting the Boss to Behave," *Business Week,* July 15, 2002, p. 110; "Auditing Here, Consulting Over There," *Business Week,* April 8, 2002, pp. 34+.

40. Jennifer Reingold, "The Gary Cooper of Governance," *Business Week,* May 29, 2000, pp. 232+.

41. Diane Brady, "If You Don't Open Your Books, We'll Cancel Your Policy," *Business Week,* August 26, 2002, p. 38; Jeremy Kahn, "Desperately Seeking Suit Protection," *Fortune,* April 1, 2002, p. 38.

42. Mike McNamee, "Will Pitt Pick an Accounting Watchdog Who Can Bite?" *Business Week,* September 2, 2002, p. 47.

43. "Why Honesty is the Best Policy;" Andy Serwer, "Dirty Rotten Numbers," *Fortune,* February 18, 2002, pp. 74+; A. Scott, "Tightening Corporate Governance," *Internal Auditor,* June 2002, pp. 13+; "Badly in Need of Repair," *The Economist,* May 4, 2002, pp. 66-68.

44. Jim Frederick, Adrienne Carter, and Stephanie D. Smith, "The Trouble with Earnings," *Money,* March 2002, pp. 72+.

45. This section draws, in part, on information in D. Larry Crumbley and Nicholas Apostolou, "Forensic Accounting: A New Growth Area in Accounting," *The Ohio CPA Journal,* July-September 2002, pp. 16+ and from Frederick, Carter, and Smith, "The Trouble with Earnings."

46. Susan Pulliam and Jared Sandberg, "New WorldCom Report to SEC Will Acknowledge More Flaws," *Wall Street Journal*, September 19, 2002, www.wsj.com; Jared Sandberg and Susan Pulliam, "WorldCom Finds More Errors; Restatement Will Be $7.2 Billion," *Wall Street Journal*, August 9, 2002, www.wsj.com.

47. Andrew Ross, "Qwest to Sell Yellow Pages for $7 Billion," *New York Times,* August 20, 2002, p. C1.

48. "19 Revenue Recognition Mistakes That Will Raise Red Flags at the SEC," *Managing the General Ledger,* June 2002, p. 10.

49. Neil Golden, "SEC Forces Rethink of Earnings Reports," *International Financial Law Review,* July 2002, pp. 19+; "Badly in Need of Repair."

50. Nanette Byrnes and Tom Lowry, "A Different Yardstick for Cable," *Business Week,* September 2, 2002, p.56; Frederick, Adrienne Carter, and Stephanie D. Smith, "The Trouble with Earnings," *Money,* March 2002, pp. 72+.

51. "Badly in Need of Repair;" D. Larry Crumbley and Nicholas Apostolou, "Forensic Accounting: A New Growth Area in Accounting," *The Ohio CPA Journal,* July-September 2002, pp. 16+.

52. Nanette Byrnes, "The Downside of Disclosure," *Business Week,* August 26, 2002, pp. 100-102; Tim Reason, "Pump Up the Volume," *CFO,* June 2002, pp. 80+; Claudia H. Deutsch, "Xerox Revises Revenue Data," *New York Times,* June 29, 2002, p. C1.

53. Ken Brown, "Auditors' Methods Make It Hard to Uncover Fraud by Executives," *Wall Street Journal,* July 8, 2002, www.wsj.com.

54. Jeremy Kahn, "One Plus One Makes What?" *Fortune,* January 7, 2002, pp. 88+; Scot J. Paltrow, "Accounting Scandals Have Some Peering At the Industry's System of Self-Policing," *Wall Street Journal,* January 14, 2002, p. A8.

55. Mike McNamee, "Out of Control at Andersen," *Business Week,* April 8, 2002, pp. 32-33; John A. Byrne, "Fall From Grace," *Business Week,* August 12, 2002, pp. 50-56; Kurt Eichenwald, "Andersen Trial Yields Evidence in Enron's Fall," *New York Times,* June 17, 2002, pp. A1+.

56. "Auditing Here, Consulting Over There," *Business Week,* April 8, 2002, pp. 34+.

57. "Expect Tougher Auditors Following the Enron Scandal," *The Controller's Report,* July 2002, pp. 1+.

58. "Enron's Wake: Controllers Can Expect End to Cozy Auditor Relationships, Warns Warren Buffett," *The Controller's Report,* July 2002, pp. 1+.

59. Louis Lavelle, "Unleashing the Watchdogs," *Business Week,* February 18, 2002, p. 40; Jonathan D. Glater, "Recomputing Earnings with Lawbook and Eraser," *New York Times,* July 2, 2002, pp. C8+.

60. Jeremy Kahn, "Practice Audits Pay Off," *Fortune,* June 24, 2002, pp. 40-42.

61. Jeffrey L. Seglin, "A Company Credo, As Applied or Not," *New York Times,* July 15, 2001, sec. 3, p. 4.

62. Del Jones, "Ethics Don't Always Pay, But Lack of Them Always Hurts," *USA Today,* July 5, 2002, www.usatoday.com.

63. Jones, "Ethics Don't Always Pay, But Lack of Them Always Hurts."

64. Marci Alboher Nusbaum, "Blowing the Whistle: Not for the Fainthearted," *New York Times,* February 10, 2002, sec. 3, p. 10.

65. Thomas Donaldson, "The Corporate Ethics Boom: Significant or Just for Show?" *Financial Times Mastering Management*, November 13, 2000, knowledge.wharton.upenn.edu/articles.cfm?articleid=285&catid=11; Gregory J. Millman, "New Scandals, Old Lessons: Financial Ethics After Enron," *Financial Executive,* July-August 2002, pp. 16+.

66. Kathryn Gordon and Maiko Miyake, "Business Approaches to Combating Bribery: A Study of Codes of Conduct," *Journal of Business Ethics* 34 (2001): pp. 161-173.

67. "Ethical Corporate Behavior Begins with a Code of Conduct," *HR Focus,* July 2002, p. 8.

68. Linda Stern, "Is Your Boss Honest?" *Newsweek,* September 23, 2002, pp. 73-74; Felo, "Ethics Programs, Board Involvement, and Potential Conflicts of Interest in Corporate Governance;" Donaldson, "The Corporate Ethics Boom."

69. Jeffrey L. Seglin, "Just Saying No to Gifts from Drug Makers," *New York Times,* August 18, 2002, sec. 3, p. 4.

70. Curtis C. Verschoor, "Were Enron's Ethical Missteps a Major Cause of Its Downfall?" *Strategic Finance,* February 2002, pp. 22+; Wee, "Corporate Ethics: Right Makes Might."

71. Millman, "New Scandals, Old Lessons;" "Dow To Give Workers Ethics Training," *Work & Family Newsbrief,* April 2002, p. 8.

72. "Dow To Give Workers Ethics Training."

73. Felo, "Ethics Programs, Board Involvement, and Potential Conflicts of Interest in Corporate Governance."

74. "Defense Contractors Create Gold Standard for Ethics Training & Compliance," *Managing Training & Development,* July 2002, pp. 1+.

75. Nusbaum, "Blowing the Whistle;" Geoffrey Colvin, "Wonder Women of Whistleblowing," *Fortune,* August 12, 2002, p. 56; Katherine Yung, "Enron Employees' Assertions Were Generally Shunted Aside," *Dallas Morning News,* July 22, 2002, www.dallasnews.com.

76. Colvin, "Wonder Women of Whistleblowing."

77. Nusbaum, "Blowing the Whistle;" Elizabeth Douglass, "California: Global Crossing Turns Over Papers to House Committee," *Los Angeles Times,* March 28, 2002, pp. C-2+.

78. Susan Orenstein, "Exposing Your Superiors for the Bunch of Rapacious, Lying Weasels That They Are: A Practical Guide," *Business 2.0,* April 2002, pp. 112-113; Nusbaum, "Blowing the Whistle."

79. Millman, "New Scandals, Old Lessons."

80. "Defense Contractors Create Gold Standard for Ethics Training and Compliance."

Chapter 3: Ethics At Enron

Introduction to Enron's Situation

Houston-based Enron filed for bankruptcy on December 2, 2001, ending a pioneering effort to profit from trading and delivering natural gas and other energy supplies in a deregulated market. Enron was born of a 1985 merger between two pipeline companies, Houston Natural Gas and InterNorth. Top management broke new ground in shaping market pricing for energy supplies, rather than operating as a staid, government-regulated utility. The company also was among the first to construct natural gas-driven electrical generating plants to provide energy for industrial customers. By 2000, Enron was reporting $101 billion in annual revenues, and its stock price was flying high because of the company's well-publicized energy trading operations. Even early on, energy trading was a prominent part of Enron's operations. However, in 1987, an oil trader in one of the New York units lost $85 million in bad trades and went to prison. Kenneth Lay, CEO at the time, called this an isolated incident, yet other questions about the company's energy trading practices cropped up in later years, as well.[1]

Meanwhile, eager to put the best possible face on finances so Enron's stock price would keep rising, management devised sophisticated ways to puff up earnings, hide losses and debts, and reduce risk. The company's auditor, Arthur Andersen, raised concerns about some of the aggressive techniques used over the years. Yet Enron's board of directors did not investigate, call a halt, or publicly disclose what was going on so analysts and investors could understand the assumptions and calculations underlying the firm's financial statements. Nor did the board object when Kenneth Lay borrowed tens of millions of dollars from the company and repaid in stock rather than cash—a losing proposition for Enron because the stock lost all value when the company went into bankruptcy.[2] The first article in this chapter, "Enron Board Accused by U.S. Senate Panel," examines the board's responsibilities in more detail.

The second article, "Officials Got a Windfall Before Enron's Collapse," discusses how dozens of Enron executives and energy traders received generous bonuses in the months before the company's bankruptcy filing, including sizable "retention bonuses" to prevent their defection to other employers. Even senior managers of a unit that was winding down shared a minimum of $10 million in bonuses. Yet thousands of ordinary employees lost their jobs because of the bankruptcy and saw the value of their retirement accounts plummet because so much of their holdings were tied up in now worthless Enron stock. In contrast, senior executives reduced their holdings of company stock by more than $1 billion in the months leading up to the bankruptcy. The courts recently cleared the way for creditors to file suit against Enron's former Chairman, CEO, CFO, and other executives and directors for breach of fiduciary duty and negligence.

The combination of Enron's bankruptcy and WorldCom's later bankruptcy has sparked new scrutiny of the checks and balances on corporate financial reporting. President Bush established a corporate crime task force to root out corporate fraud. In the task force's first 10 weeks, it looked into 100 cases of potential fraud, charged over 150 defendants, and received convictions or plea agreements in 46 cases. The FBI has assigned 2,000 agents to investigate white-collar crime, and the SEC has beefed up its enforcement staff by 50 employees. Some of Enron's senior managers are already facing federal charges and others may be indicted in the near future. For example, former CFO Andrew Fastow has been charged with fraud, money laundering, and conspiracy for allegedly directing complex schemes to inflate profits and conceal debts. Throughout 2003, the final chapter in Enron's history will continue unfolding in courtrooms rather than on the energy trading floor.[3]

"Enron Board Accused by U.S. Senate Panel," by Kelly Patricia O'Meara

With the recent record bankruptcy filing by WorldCom Inc., the Houston-based Enron Corp., formerly the seventh-largest corporation in America, no longer holds the dubious distinction of being the nation's No. 1 corporate failure. That's the good news … and the bad news.

Most believe these corporate crashes are just the tip of an enormous iceberg that has been struck by the titanic U.S. economy. Often the bankrupt behemoths are referred to in press accounts as having been "felled" by accounting scandals, as if bean counters in suspenders and green eyeshades mistakenly had put a few zeros in the wrong columns. But a quietly released Senate report reviewed by *INSIGHT* reveals what accountants and auditors long have known – that figures don't lie but liars figure.

Immediately following the December 2001 bankruptcy filing of Enron, the Senate Permanent subcommittee on Investigations chaired by Carl Levin (D-Mich.) conducted an in-depth investigation into the collapse of the highly touted oil and gas company. Over a six-month period the subcommittee issued more than 50 subpoenas, reviewed the contents of more than 350 boxes of related documents and interviewed 13 past and present Enron board members. The subcommittee concluded that the Enron board of directors could not escape its responsibility – that the board had, according to the Business Roundtable, failed in its "paramount duty" to safeguard the interest of the company's shareholders. The subcommittee findings are as follows:

- **Fiduciary failure.** The Enron board failed to safeguard Enron shareholders and contributed to the collapse of the seventh-largest public company in the United States by allowing it to engage in high-risk accounting, inappropriate conflict-of-interest transactions, extensive undisclosed off-the-books activities and excessive executive compensation. The board witnessed numerous indications of questionable practices by Enron management over several years but chose to ignore them to the detriment of company shareholders, employees and business associates.

- **High-risk accounting.** The board knowingly allowed the company to engage in high-risk accounting practices.

- **Inappropriate conflicts of interest.** Despite clear conflicts of interest, the board approved an unprecedented arrangement allowing Enron's chief financial officer (CFO) to establish and operate the LJM private equity funds that transacted business with Enron and profited at Enron's expense. The board exercised inadequate oversight of LJM transaction and compensation controls and failed to protect Enron shareholders from unfair dealing.

- **Extensive undisclosed off-the-books activity.** The board knowingly allowed the company to conduct billions of dollars in off-the-books activity to make its financial condition appear better than it was. The board also failed to ensure adequate public disclosure of material off-the-books liabilities that contributed to Enron's collapse.

- **Excessive compensation.** The board approved excessive compensation for company executives, failed to monitor the cumulative cash drain caused by Enron's 2000 annual bonus and performance-unit plans, and failed to monitor or halt abuse by chairman and chief executive officer (CEO) Kenneth Lay of a company-financed, multimillion-dollar, personal credit line.

- **Lack of independence.** The independence of Enron's board was compromised by financial ties between the company and certain board members. The board also failed to ensure the independence of the company's auditor, allowing the Arthur Andersen accounting firm to provide internal audit and consulting services while serving as Enron's outside auditor.

In a nutshell, the subcommittee found that the Enron board of directors failed to safeguard the company's shareholders, engaged in high-risk accounting, allowed numerous inappropriate conflict-of-interest transactions, was fully aware of and allowed off-the-books activities, and granted excessive compensation.

Based on in-depth interviews with board members and the review of millions of documents, the subcommittee was not persuaded that the downfall of Enron was due to inadvertent accounting mistakes. Rather, the subcommittee's monthslong investigation suggests that the board not only had knowledge of Enron's complicated yet deteriorating financial transactions, but continued to give its blessings up to the point of the corporate implosion.

The subcommittee reported that Enron board members were compensated with cash, restricted stock, phantom stock units and stock options totaling $350,000 a year – more than twice the national average for large publicly traded companies. For this lofty sum, the subcommittee further reports, the board members who were interviewed admitted to spending on average between two and 16 hours preparing for board meetings, which were scheduled five times a year.

Assuming the average time spent preparing for a board meeting was eight hours for each session, and each spent 12 hours in travel and attendance, the total is 20 hours per meeting. Another way to examine the data is that the members of the board spent 100 hours per year on board meetings and were paid $3,500 per hour, or $70,000 per meeting.

According to the subcommittee, board members were fully aware of the coming implosion. "From October until the company's bankruptcy on Dec. 2, 2001, the board held numerous special meetings, at times on an almost daily basis." While the evidence collected by the subcommittee points to board responsibility for Enron's collapse, Enron's directors, according to the report, "seemed to indicate that they were as surprised as anyone by the company's collapse."

The subcommittee didn't buy the directors' claims not to know what was going on and provided information about more than a dozen incidents over three years that should have alarmed any responsible board. While the subcommittee acknowledged some instances where the board was misinformed or misled, the investigation found "that overall the board received substantial information about Enron's plans and activities and explicitly authorized or allowed many of the questionable Enron strategies, policies and transactions now subject to criticism." For instance, according to the Senate subcommittee investigation report:
  • Enron's high-risk accounting practices were not hidden; rather, the board knew of them and took no action to prevent the risky activity.
  • The board was briefed on the purpose and nature of the highly dubious Whitewing, LJM and Raptor transactions, explicitly approved them and received updates on their operations.
  • Enron's extensive off-the-books activity (offshore accounts) not only was well known to the board, but was made possible by board resolutions authorizing new unconsolidated entities, Enron preferred shares and Enron stock collateral featured in many of the off-the-books deals.

Despite being faced with evidence indicating otherwise during interviews with the subcommittee, board members continued to blame underlings and outside consultants. For example, John Duncan, former chairman of the Enron executive committee, which was tasked with "handling urgent business matters," told the subcommittee that "the board worked hard and asked probing questions." Duncan also claimed the problem at Enron was that management did not "tell the truth." He contended that both Enron management and Arthur Andersen personnel "were well aware of the problems facing the company and did not tell us."

Herbert "Pug" Winokur – the former head of Enron's finance committee who also sits on half-a-dozen other boards, including DynCorp – testified that what happened to Enron is "a cautionary reminder of the limits of a director's role," which is by nature a "part-time job." He further stated, "We cannot, I submit, be criticized for failing to address or remedy problems that have been concealed from us," ignoring the fact that the directors were paid $70,000 for 20 hours of work to watch for risky practices. The employees and shareholders of Enron who lost hundreds of millions of dollars weren't informed that Winokur's presence on the board meant nothing because it was just a "part-time" job.

The senators certainly didn't acknowledge such excuses, observing: "The subcommittee investigation did not substantiate the claims that the board members challenged management and asked tough questions. Instead, the investigation found a board that routinely relied on Enron management and Andersen representatives with little or no effort to verify the information provided." The senators concluded that "the failure of any Enron board member to accept any degree of personal responsibility for Enron's collapse is a telling indicator of the board's failure to recognize its fiduciary obligations to set the company's overall strategic direction, oversee management and ensure responsible financial reporting."

Although the subcommittee report notes numerous examples of bizarre financial arrangements approved by the board, one personal transaction involving Lay seems to be evidence of very sophisticated knowledge on the part of the board. In May 1999, the board of directors allowed Lay to repay company loans with stock. By August 2001 – four months before the company crashed – the line of credit approved by the board to Lay had increased to $7.5 million. Lay used that line of credit, according to one board member, as though it were an ATM.

Indeed, Lay used the "credit line" to remove more than $77 million in cash from the company and repaid the "loan" with Enron stock, which within months would be worthless. The board members who were interviewed claimed to be unaware of these transactions. The $77 million was withdrawn from the company by the CEO and repaid with stock yet, the subcommittee says, the board was "unaware" of the transactions?

The Enron board was composed of 15 members and divided into five committees. Each member was well educated and had decades of experience. All were considered experts in areas of finance and accounting, were successful in business and held positions on other corporate boards. Each knew millions of Americans had invested their money in Enron on the assumption that the company was run with good business practices and that the men and women at the top were responsible managers, alert, in control and fully aware of the company's financial situation. But the subcommittee found that the directors were irresponsible or worse. And with Enron being only the first in a long line of corporations being "felled" by accounting scandals, the outcome for its managers and directors likely will make it the poster child for the public and legal consequences that follow in other corporations.

But the subcommittee, rather than suggest criminal investigations and indictments, recommended only legislative and regulatory changes, already under way in half-a-dozen committees on Capitol Hill and in federal regulatory agencies that oversee the financial and accounting sectors.

Will the men who condoned fraud and other crimes and pocketed enormous gains get away with it like the robber barons of the Gilded Age? Sen. Conrad Burns (R-Mont.) believes the "part-time" corporate board members of these erring corporations should be handled no differently than drug kingpins. Eric Bovin, director of communications for Burns, tells *INSIGHT* that "the senator is on the trail," convinced that "if you commit a crime – defrauding people for profit – then you deserve to have your assets seized. It's that simple, and he's requested recommendations from the Department of Justice on the legal how of it. The legislation will do one thing and one thing alone. If you're convicted of a crime, and you're an executive of a publicly traded company, your ill-gotten second homes, toys and fancy assets will be seized."

Tough talk. But how will other indictments come down to match the Justice Department's arrest of the Rigas family and executives charged with looting Adelphia Communications? The subcommittee reports a low interest of law enforcement in those responsible for the Enron crash. "During April 2002, the subcommittee staff interviewed 13 past and present Enron board members, none of whom had previously been interviewed by the U.S. Department of Justice, Federal Bureau of Investigation or the Securities and Exchange Commission." Nearly five months after Enron filed for bankruptcy, no one in law enforcement had even talked with the board members. *INSIGHT* asked Brian Sierra, a Justice Department spokesman, about this. His response: "We can't talk about those details. It's an ongoing investigation."

With the market fighting a panic, many are wondering when Justice Department investigators will find time to talk to the men and women who ran Enron. Surely enforcing the law, these critics say, is not a part-time job.

"Officials Got a Windfall Before Enron's Collapse," by David Barboza

In the year before the Enron Corporation collapsed last December, about 100 executives and energy traders collected more than $300 million in cash payments from the company, according to documents filed today in bankruptcy court.

More than $100 million -- much of it previously disclosed in the form of salary, bonuses and loans -- went to Kenneth L. Lay, the company's former chairman and chief executive.

A majority of the cash payments went to employees of units whose profitability has been called into question since the company's collapse. In Enron's energy-trading unit, for example, John J. Lavorato, a top executive, and John D. Arnold, a gas trader, each received cash bonuses of $8 million to keep them from leaving Enron last fall.

Enron's trading unit generated the bulk of the company's profits in 2000 and 2001, and as a result, its executives and traders received a majority of the $50 million in retention bonuses the company agreed to pay just ahead of the bankruptcy filing.

But according to former Enron executives, the trading division relied heavily on so-called mark-to-market accounting to value its trading positions, booking revenue from long-term contracts immediately. Investigations of the unit's profits and revenue could call into question the trading unit's success and the cash bonuses made to traders for profits that the company was not expected to realize for years. The bankruptcy filing is also notable for its payments to executives in the broadband division, a unit that was being phased out in early 2001. Still, top executives in the faltering division took in at least $10 million in bonuses.

The disclosure of scores of large cash payments is certain to increase the ire of former lower-level employees who have long complained about how high-level executives sold more than $1 billion in Enron shares in the year before the company filed for bankruptcy protection.

Thousands of Enron workers were laid off after the filing on Dec. 2, and many have complained that they got little in severance pay and lost millions of dollars they had put into the company's 401(k) retirement accounts.

Yet even as the company was hurtling toward bankruptcy, some valued traders and executives were showered with huge retention bonuses worth nearly $100 million, according to the documents.

The company's top executives also were paid huge cash payments, mostly in the form of bonuses and long-term incentive pay. For instance, Jeffrey K. Skilling, who resigned as chief executive last August, received $7.5 million in cash bonuses and incentive pay; Mr. Lay got $10.6 million in similar payments. David W. Delainey, a former Enron Energy Services executive, received $4.2 million.

"I am appalled at the money that was given to these top executives," said Mary Wyatt, a former Enron executive who lost about $500,000 in deferred compensation after the company collapsed.

Richard Rathvon, a former employee who is co-chairman of the employee committee in the bankruptcy case, said that he was still studying the documents. But his group is seeking to recover some of the huge bonuses paid to Enron executives who later left the company.

Enron, which is struggling to emerge from bankruptcy protection, has agreed to work with the employee group to recover some of the money it paid in bonuses last year.

In recent weeks, Enron has sent letters to former employees requesting the repayment of some of that bonus money. But Enron officials say the company is not going to recover the money itself but will pass on information to the employee group.

Meanwhile, the Senate Finance Committee said today that it was looking into whether top executives at Enron had placed their bonuses in offshore accounts and had later withdrawn that money without paying federal taxes.

The investigation, part of the committee's inquiry into Enron's tax payments going back to 1985, is still in its early stages, but investigators suspect that some executives, perhaps with the help of Enron, may have engaged in tax evasion.

"We're looking into the possibility that senior executives at Enron may have taken corporate bonuses, withdrawn these bonuses and not reported them as taxable income," said Michael A. Siegel, a spokesman for the Senate Finance Committee.

Creditors are also scrutinizing Enron's filing today in the bankruptcy court in New York. They will be poring over hundreds of pages detailing large payments to an array of banks and corporations in the months leading up to the bankruptcy.

Andrew Entwistle, who represents the Florida State pension fund, said creditors and the bankruptcy trustee would be looking into whether Enron had made preferential payments to certain banks and other companies.

Among the major payments Enron made in the months ahead of the bankruptcy filing were a $13 million payment to the company's auditor, Arthur Andersen; $19 million to Morgan Stanley; $16 million to Salomon Smith Barney; and $215 million to Credit Suisse First Boston.

An Enron official, however, said that some of the large payments, including one for $349 million to UBS Warburg, might have been related to foreign currency exchange.

The bankruptcy filing is also notable for its payments to executives in the broadband division, which was being phased out in early 2001. Wall Street analysts say the unit never took off and lost millions of dollars. Still, its top executives took in at least $10 million in bonuses in 2001.

Most of the bonuses detailed in the long bankruptcy filing, which included more than 1,000 pages of financial documents, were made in early 2001, based on work done in 2000, when shares of Enron were soaring.

Now federal investigators are looking into whether Enron executives inflated profits and hid debt to drive up the share price so top executives could meet performance goals.

Altogether, the company's top executives earned more than $600 million in salaries, bonuses, incentives and stock in 2001. Much of the stock, though, proved worthless near the end of the year.

The rapid decline in the stock price in 2001 forced Mr. Lay to borrow money from Enron and to liquidate other investments to avoid margin calls on a variety of banks loans. Those loans had been collateralized with Enron stock. He repaid Enron by relinquishing some of his Enron shares to the company, according to Kelly Kimberly, a spokeswoman for Mr. Lay.

The documents released today show that Mr. Lay borrowed about $80 million from Enron in the year before the collapse. Ms. Kimberly said most of that loan had been repaid.

What is interesting about the filing today, though, is that while executives like Mr. Lay and Mr. Skilling were highly compensated, many of the highest-paid employees were from the trading unit.

Phillip K. Allen, who worked on the gas desk on the West Coast, received a $4.4 million bonus; Timothy Belden, an executive on the power desk in Portland, Ore., got a $5.2 million bonus. And Mr. Arnold, who made about $700 million in trading profits for Enron in 2001, largely by trading gas on the West Coast, was paid the biggest bonus, $8 million.

"Officials Got a Windfall Before Enron's Collapse" by David Barboza, The New York Times, June 18, 2002. Copyright © 2002 by the New York Times Co. Reprinted by permission.

Questions For Discussion, Analysis, and Further Research

1. *For discussion and analysis:* Based on the information in Chapters 1 and 2 and the articles included in this chapter, how did Enron's corporate governance practices—particularly the involvement of its board of directors—seem to affect the company's ability to adequately address internal ethical concerns? As your instructor directs, respond to this question individually, as part of a student team, or through participation in a classroom discussion.

2. *For discussion and analysis:* Should Enron's board of directors have protected the interests of shareholders as its highest priority? If not, which other stakeholder group—management, employees, or another stakeholder group—should have been the board's highest priority? Explain your answer.

3. *For debate:* Should directors be required to own shares in a company's stock as a condition of participating in the board? Or should directors be prevented from owning more than a token holding of company shares to avoid a potential conflict of interest? Support your position using information from Chapters 1 and 2 as well as the articles in this chapter, supplemented with outside research if needed.

4. *For further research:* The value of many Enron employees' 401(k) retirement accounts dropped precipitously as the company moved into bankruptcy, because company policy forced employees to hold shares for long periods before being allowed to sell. Employees could do nothing but watch as the shares in their retirement accounts lost value day after day. What legal and regulatory changes are currently being considered or enacted to prevent such occurrences in the future? What changes would you recommend? Use Internet or library sources to research this question, then present your findings and position in a written or oral report.

REFERENCES

1. Toni Mack, "The Other Enron Story," *Forbes,* October 14, 2002, pp. 62+; Bethany McLean, "Monster Mess: The Enron Fallout Has Just Begun," *Fortune,* February 4, 2002, pp. 93+.

2. Reed Abelson, "Enron Board Comes Under a Storm of Criticism," *New York Times,* December 16, 2001, sec. 3, p. 4; Kelly Patricia O'Meara, "Enron Board Accused by U.S. Senate Panel," *Insight,* August 19, 2002, pp. 15-17.

3. Mitchell Pacelle and Kathryn Kranhold, "Enron Creditors Get Approval for Suit Against Ex-Executives," *Wall Street Journal*, October 2, 2002, www.wsj.com; David Barboza, "Officials Got a Windfall Before Enron's Collapse," *New York Times,* June 18, 2002, pp. 3+; John R. Wilke, "President Praises Work Done by Business-Crime Task Force," *Wall Street Journal*, September 27, 2002, www.wsj.com.

Chapter 4: Ethics At Arthur Andersen

Introduction to Arthur Andersen's Situation

Arthur Andersen, the public accounting firm that audited the financial reports of Enron and WorldCom—among thousands of other public companies—was founded in 1913 by a Northwestern University accounting professor. The firm concentrated on auditing until it began consulting on technology projects in 1954. During 2000, the consulting side paid $1 billion to break free from the auditing side and start life independently under the Accenture name. By 2001, the auditing group (which retained the Arthur Andersen name) had 85,000 employees in offices around the world and was bringing in $9.3 billion in annual revenues. After the split with Accenture, Andersen moved aggressively to generate more revenue from consulting projects.[1]

Meanwhile, Arthur Andersen became embroiled in controversies over its auditing work for several clients. For example, in 2001, the SEC extracted a $7 million penalty because Andersen failed to detect $1.1 billion in income overstatements by client Waste Management; in addition, Andersen paid almost $100 million to settle shareholders' claims in the case. Another client, Sunbeam, managed to overstate its net income by $71.1 million, and later declared bankruptcy; Andersen paid $110 million in 2001 to settle the claims of Sunbeam shareholders. In neither of these cases did Andersen admit guilt when settling the legal actions.[2]

Enron was also a client. After the energy company sought bankruptcy protection in December, 2001, government investigators asked pointed questions about Andersen's interactions with Enron's management. Andersen's lawyers began searching internally for evidence and noticed that thousands of e-mails and documents had been destroyed. This set off a chain of events that resulted in a former Andersen partner pleading guilty to obstruction of justice for his role in the destruction and, ultimately, to Andersen's mid-2002 conviction (as an organization) for obstructing justice in the SEC's investigation of Enron's financial woes.[3] The first article in this chapter, "Andersen Guilty in Effort to Block Inquiry on Enron," explains this conviction.

WorldCom's bankruptcy filing in 2002 brought kept Andersen in the spotlight. Andersen had reportedly assured WorldCom's audit committee that the telecommunications company had adequate procedures for detecting accounting irregularities—yet a series of multimillion dollar misstatements led WorldCom to repeatedly restate its financial reports.[4] The second article in this chapter, "Auditor Gave Assurances of Safeguards Against Fraud," discusses this aspect of the WorldCom situation.

Andersen faced still more litigation in 2002. Peregrine Systems, a software company, sued for over $1 billion, charging that Andersen's failure to notify the audit committee about improper accounting contributed to the company's bankruptcy filing. "Arthur Andersen was aware that there was trouble," stated one of Peregrine's lawyers. "Their client is the auditing committee, and they failed to tell the committee or the board what was really going on." An Andersen spokesperson responded, "Responsibility for bad business decisions lies with the board and their management team. This lawsuit is clearly an effort to divert attention from the company's own missteps."[5]

By September, 2002, Andersen had surrendered its auditing licenses in all 50 states and reduced its U.S. workforce by more than 23,000 employees. Competitors paid Andersen an average of $100,000 per partner to hire away thousands of the firm's accounting experts. Although the company vowed to continue operating in some form, it faced a daunting number of lawsuits and had lost all its auditing clients. Its future remains uncertain.[6]

"Andersen Guilty in Effort to Block Inquiry on Enron," by Kurt Eichenwald

A federal jury convicted Arthur Andersen today of obstruction of justice for impeding an investigation by securities regulators into the financial debacle at Enron. Soon afterward, Andersen informed the government that it would cease auditing public companies as soon as the end of August, effectively ending the life of the 89-year-old firm.

The jury verdict, reached in the 10th day of deliberations, reflected a narrow reading of the events last fall that led to Andersen's indictment. In interviews, jurors said that they reached their decision because an Andersen lawyer had ordered critical deletions to an internal memorandum, rather than because of the firm's wholesale destruction of Enron-related documents.

At bottom, then, the guilty verdict against Andersen -- on a charge brought because of the shredding of thousands of records and deletion of tens of thousands of e-mail messages -- was ultimately reached because of the removal of a few words from a single memorandum.

The conviction is the first ever against a major accounting firm and was based on the first criminal indictment stemming from the government's investigation into the events that led to Enron's collapse in December. Sentencing has been scheduled for Oct. 11, and Andersen faces the possibility of fines up to $500,000.

With Andersen already failing, and the firm having given up on its effort to emerge from the scandal as a model for reforming the accounting profession, the most important result of the verdict was that it closed the books on the firm's hopes of surviving even in a reduced state. Within hours of the verdict, the Securities and Exchange Commission issued a statement that Andersen was voluntarily relinquishing its ability to audit public companies in the United States, a privilege that requires authorization to practice before the agency.

"The commission is deeply troubled by the underlying events that resulted in Andersen's conviction, especially insofar as the verdict reflects the jury's conclusion that Andersen engaged in conduct designed to obstruct S.E.C. processes," the agency said in its statement. "In light of the jury verdict and the underlying events, Andersen has informed the commission that it will cease practicing before the commission by Aug. 31, 2002, unless the commission determines another date is appropriate."

Andersen is already a shell of its former self. The firm has lost 690 of its 2,311 public company clients since Jan. 1. It has shrunk from 27,000 employees in the United States to 10,000 at most, between layoffs and the departures of whole offices and practices to competing firms.

Rusty Hardin, Andersen's lead lawyer in the case, said that the firm would appeal the conviction, which would most likely take more than a year to wind its way through the courts, meaning that the outcome would have little effect on Andersen's ability to survive.

The guilty verdict came this morning after a criminal trial of almost six weeks that had frequently been slow and complex, punctuated by sometimes fiery closing arguments from the prosecution and the defense.

Prosecutors, who have been harshly criticized by Andersen and its supporters for bringing a case that crippled the firm, said that the verdict underscored the significance of the crime and provided an important lesson to an accounting industry struggling under the weight of almost daily financial scandals.

"The verdict sends a message out loud and clear to the accounting industry to get their priorities straight," said Samuel W. Buell, an assistant United States attorney who was one of the prosecutors. Andersen, Mr. Buell said, was working too hard to protect itself and Enron, its client, without enough attention to the interests of the investing public.

Andrew Weissmann, another lead prosecutor on the case, said the verdict also showed that employees upset about the firm's collapse "should look to Andersen management" for responsibility for the debacle. The indictment of Andersen came after the firm or its representatives had already faced litigation from the S.E.C. over accounting failures involving other clients, Waste Management and the Sunbeam Corporation. "This was a management team that already had two strikes against them," Mr. Weissmann said. "And they refused to take this situation seriously."

But Andersen and its lawyers reacted to the verdict with strong disappointment, maintaining that the firm never committed a crime in its destruction of Enron documents.

"We do not regret going to trial," C.E. Andrews, a senior partner at the firm who attended the proceedings, said outside the courthouse. "The purpose of this is to fight for our honor and dignity. We do not believe we committed a crime."

Mr. Hardin, Andersen's lead lawyer in the case, said that, in describing the rationale behind its verdict, the jury members demonstrated that they had rejected the government's primary accusations against the firm -- namely, that the large scale destruction of records last fall was undertaken for the purpose of impeding a preliminary inquiry by the S.E.C. into Enron's finances.

"They convicted on a theory that wasn't even argued by the government," Mr. Hardin said. "After 10 days, they could never conclude that this evidence supported the allegation that Arthur Andersen destroyed documents to keep them away from the S.E.C."

Mr. Hardin said that the narrow basis of the decision -- involving revisions in a document that was preserved and turned over to the government -- could have a damaging effect across corporate America.

"If in fact what they chose means we're guilty of a crime, then every corporation in America ought to just cringe with fear," he said.

The verdict came after days of debate over a jury question, which resulted in a precedent-setting ruling on Friday by the judge in the case, Melinda F. Harmon of Federal District Court, that supported the prosecution. In response to a question from the jurors, she decided that they could find the firm guilty even if they could not agree on which of the firm's employees had the intent to commit the crime.

But jurors said today that they had ultimately agreed on a single Andersen partner as having had the intent to impede the S.E.C. inquiry. That partner, Nancy Temple, a lawyer with the firm's legal department, was a central participant in a series of discussions last fall about Enron and Andersen's response to the company's financial troubles.

The critical piece of evidence, the jurors said, was an internal memorandum written in mid-October of last year by David B. Duncan, the lead partner on the Enron account. The draft of that memorandum portrayed a conversation Mr. Duncan had with Richard A. Causey, Enron's chief accounting officer, about a news release the energy company was planning to issue regarding its third-quarter earnings. That release characterized certain losses Enron was reporting as "nonrecurring;" at the time, several Andersen experts, including Mr. Duncan, had concluded that such a representation was misleading.

In his conversation, Mr. Duncan told Mr. Causey that such misleading information issued by other companies in the past had resulted in actions by the S.E.C. His draft memorandum of that conversation dutifully chronicled that portion of the discussion. But, on review, Ms. Temple suggested that Mr. Duncan remove that portion of the memorandum from the final draft, and Mr. Duncan did so.

Oscar Criner, the foreman of the jury, referred to that memorandum as the smoking gun, and said that the jury concluded Ms. Temple made her suggestions for the purpose of keeping the information from the S.E.C. As such,

Mr. Criner and other jurors said, the jury agreed that Ms. Temple had "corruptly persuaded" Mr. Duncan to alter information for the purpose of impeding an official proceeding. For that reason, they said, they voted to convict.

Under that rationale, Mr. Duncan, who has already pleaded guilty to obstruction, did not engage in a crime in making the revisions.

Andersen was charged with obstructing an S.E.C. investigation by destroying thousands of records related to its audit of Enron.

The prosecution argued that Andersen made a deliberate effort to prevent outside parties, including the S.E.C., from learning the full story about Enron's accounting. But the defense countered that the government had failed to provide any proof that anyone at Andersen had acted with corrupt intent to impede an inquiry.

According to testimony at the trial, the roots of the Andersen case emerged last year, as the growing financial problems at Enron were beginning to come to light. In August, members of the firm's Enron audit team sent memorandums to Andersen's accounting specialists in Chicago, describing consultations that they had months before about a group of partnerships known as the Raptors.

But the accounting specialists found that the memorandums did not accurately reflect the consultations and that Enron's accounting procedures had been specifically determined by the specialists to violate generally accepted accounting principles.

As the two sides discussed what the memorandums should say, it was becoming evident that this accounting dispute could have enormous financial repercussions on Enron. At about that point, the legal department at Andersen became involved in the discussions. Eventually, by late September, the matter was assigned to Ms. Temple, a relatively new lawyer in the department.

As the discussions continued, more problems with the Enron accounting began to emerge. Rapidly, it became evident that the company was facing a potential financial debacle. By Oct. 8, Ms. Temple began to discuss Andersen's document-retention policy in a series of conference calls with other members of the firm.

This policy required that final memorandums and documents be placed in the work papers maintained by the accountants, while all other records -- including e-mail messages, notes and draft memorandums -- be destroyed.

On Oct. 12, Ms. Temple sent an e-mail message to Houston, saying that "it would be helpful" if members of the accounting team working on Enron made sure that they were in compliance with the document-retention policy.

On Oct. 17, soon after Enron's financial problems first became public, the S.E.C. sent a letter to the company saying that an informal inquiry into some financial practices had begun. Andersen learned of the letter two days later. Days later, on Oct. 23, Mr. Duncan instructed members of his team to comply with the document policy. Those instructions were repeated in the days that followed. In response, thousands of e-mail messages were deleted, and dozens of trunks full of documents were sent to the shredders.

In the weeks that followed, the Enron debacle escalated, ending with the company's filing for bankruptcy protection in December. Congress began its investigations, and Andersen was on the hot seat. In early January, as lawyers for the firm were examining laptop computers for e-mail messages related to Enron, they discovered that the records had been wiped clean. Soon, top Andersen executives learned of the huge effort to destroy documents.

Andersen alerted the S.E.C., the Justice Department and the Congressional committees investigating Enron. Within days, it determined that Mr. Duncan had improperly engaged in a destruction effort and fired him. In testimony before Congress late in January, a senior Andersen official said all evidence pointed to the fact that Mr. Duncan was destroying records to keep them away from investigators.

By early March, the government decided how it would handle the matter.

Based largely on what had happened in the conference calls, and on the evidence of Ms. Temple's actions, prosecutors determined that the document destruction was a coordinated effort led from Chicago, and thus merited the indictment of Andersen.

"Andersen Guilty in Effort To Block Inquiry on Enron" by Kurt Eichenwald, The New York Times, June 16, 2002. Copyright © 2002 by the New York Times Co. Reprinted by permission.

"Auditor Gave Assurances of Safeguards Against Fraud," by Kurt Eichenwald

Arthur Andersen assured WorldCom's audit committee in February that the company had strict procedures in place to prevent false statements in financial filings -- even in areas that proved to be central to the company's bookkeeping scandal, according to a copy of Andersen's report.

The report to the audit committee, provided as an exhibit in a WorldCom filing yesterday with the Securities and Exchange Commission, also assured WorldCom's directors that there had been no significant changes in the accounting policies during 2001. That was the year that the company's management adopted new procedures for handling expenses, ultimately resulting in $3.8 billion of misstatements in the financial records.

The WorldCom filing to the S.E.C. was submitted to explain the events surrounding the discovery of the false expense reports at the company. The statement was an expanded version of an earlier explanation that the S.E.C. chairman, Harvey L. Pitt, had criticized as inadequate.

The statement and attached exhibits offered slightly more detail about those events, many of which have been previously reported. For example, the statement confirmed that Scott D. Sullivan, WorldCom's former chief financial officer who orchestrated the expense shifts that led to the financial misstatements, tried to persuade an internal company auditor to postpone a review of those expense items until later this year. The auditor, Cynthia Cooper, nonetheless continued with the audit.

The report also suggests that the audit that uncovered the improper expense accounting had been set in motion by Mr. Sullivan himself. It cites -- without contradiction -- a statement by Mr. Sullivan that he had "originated the request for Ms. Cooper's review," but that he had asked her to hold off a quarter "to allow him to address the situation."

In addition, the statement details a disagreement last month that briefly pitted Ms. Cooper against an outside accountant and the head of WorldCom's audit committee, Max Bobbitt. The outside accountant, Farrell Malone of KPMG, had been appointed to head his firm's team on WorldCom a short time before, after Andersen was replaced as the company's accountant.

On June 13 -- the day after Ms. Cooper informed both men of her preliminary findings -- she told them that the details should be turned over immediately to the audit committee, which was meeting the next day. But Mr. Bobbitt and Mr. Malone of KPMG said that they believed that such a move would be premature, because the internal audit had not yet been completed. Mr. Bobbitt did not inform other members of the audit committee until six days later, after a series of other interviews of WorldCom executives had been conducted.

The critical turning point in the audit, according to the filed statement, was on June 18, when Mr. Malone interviewed David F. Myers, then the controller of the company. During that discussion, the statement says, Mr. Myers indicated that huge expense transfers had been made into the capital expenditures portion of the books in the previous five quarters without any support for the accounting. Essentially, that interview established that the expense transfers were not handled as normal accounting adjustments would have been.

The details about Andersen's advice raise questions about whether the firm had simply been sloppy in its assessments, or whether standard auditing practices are so ineffectual that a potential fraud of almost $4 billion could go undetected, even when the areas involved are reviewed.

Andersen maintains that its work was professional and appropriate at all times, and senior Andersen officials say that the firm was simply the victim of deceit by WorldCom's management.

In the course of their report to the WorldCom audit committee, the Andersen accountants also assured the directors that there had been no significant or unusual transactions in 2001 -- the very time when billions of dollars in costs were being shifted between operating expenses and capital expenses, a move that improperly inflated the company's reported profits.

Questions For Discussion, Analysis, and Further Research

1. *For discussion and analysis:* Based on the information in Chapters 1 and 2 and the articles included in this chapter, should Arthur Andersen have been found guilty, as an organization, of obstructing justice during the Enron inquiry? As your instructor directs, respond to this question individually, as part of a student team, or through participation in a classroom discussion.

2. *For discussion and analysis:* Against her manager's wishes, an internal auditor at WorldCom uncovered irregularities that offered clues to a larger pattern of mischaracterizing expenses to make earnings look better. What might a company do to encourage employees to report incidences of suspected fraud, even when the reports implicate their direct supervisors or others higher in the chain of command? Explain your answer.

3. *For debate:* Should public companies be allowed to sue the accounting firms that audit their financial reports if serious accounting irregularities or fraudulent actions are later found? Support your position using information from Chapters 1 and 2 as well as the articles in this chapter, supplemented with outside research if needed.

4. *For further research:* Changing accounting firms can result in higher auditing costs because the new firm must start from scratch in learning about the company's accounting policies and procedures. On the other hand, new auditors often suggest new ways for their clients to prevent potential problems. Use Internet or library sources to research how one or two clients of Andersen handled the transition when switching to new auditors. Summarize the challenges and opportunities these companies faced in a written or oral report.

REFERENCES

---

1. John A. Byrne, "Fall From Grace," *Business Week,* August 12, 2002, pp. 50-56; "Andersen's Bad Experience Yields Sobering Lessons," *USA Today,* April 12, 2002, www.usatoday.com.

2. Byrne, "Fall From Grace;" "Andersen's Bad Experience."

3. Kurt Eichenwald, "Miscues, Missteps and the Fall of Andersen," *New York Times,* May 8, 2002, pp. C1+.

4. Kurt Eichenwald, "Auditor Gave Assurances of Safeguards Against Fraud," *New York Times,* July 9, 2002, pp. C5+.

5. P.J. Huffstutter, "Peregrine Sues Arthur Andersen," *Los Angeles Times,* September 24, 2002, pp. C1+.

6. Karen Robinson-Jacobs, "Andersen Says Goodbye to Accounting," *Los Angeles Times,* August 31, 2002, pp. C1+; "Corporate Accountability," *Wall Street Journal*, August 6, 2002, www.wsj.com.

Chapter 5: Ethics At WorldCom

Introduction to WorldCom's Situation

WorldCom was once a powerful force in the telecommunications industry. Founded in 1983 as

LDDS Communications, the fast-growing company swallowed up MCI—then the second-largest

U.S. long-distance telephone carrier—and eventually controlled a significant percentage of the

U.S. Internet backbone. The stock price soared to over $60 per share during the heyday of the

bear market in mid-1999. Behind the scenes, however, WorldCom's management felt intense

pressure to sustain rapid growth year after year while reporting profits despite a highly

competitive marketplace. Moreover, the firm was buried under a multibillion-dollar mound of

debt from numerous acquisitions. Throughout 2001 and into 2002, as the industry coped with

price wars, a sluggish economy, and other major challenges, the stock price slid lower and lower.

In March, 2002, as the SEC began digging deeper into WorldCom's accounting practices,

the company announced worldwide layoffs to reduce spending. Soon management faced

questions about $366 million in loans made to founder Bernard J. Ebbers, who used the funds to

buy company stock; he stepped down as CEO on April 30. At the end of June, the SEC charged

WorldCom with illegally padding earnings by $3.8 billion. The stock price had dropped below

$1 by the time WorldCom declared bankruptcy in July, 2002, in the largest filing in U.S. history

to that point. Even after the bankruptcy, WorldCom continued to identify billions of dollars in

accounting irregularities.[1] See the first article, "WorldCom Files for Bankruptcy; Largest U.S.

Case," for more background on this bankruptcy.

What happened? Investigations are continuing, but according to former controller David

F. Myers, "senior management" issued instructions to "falsify WorldCom's books, to reduce

WorldCom's reported actual costs and therefore increase WorldCom's reported earnings."[2] Arthur Andersen was paid more than $4 million yearly to check on WorldCom's financial reports, but its auditors apparently never discovered how earnings were inflated by a relatively simple accounting trick: classifying routine operating expenses (which are usually deducted from current income) as capital expenses (which are deducted from income in smaller chunks over a number of years). Although this procedure does not follow GAAP, WorldCom used it month after month to minimize expenses and thereby manage to report earnings that met Wall Street's expectations and kept the stock price up. Eventually, the company revealed it had uncovered more than $7 billion in misstated expenses.[3] See the second article, "WorldCom Accounting Debacle Shows How Easy Fraud Can Be," for more on WorldCom's accounting.

David Myers later pleaded guilty to securities fraud, conspiracy to commit securities fraud, and filing false SEC reports. His cooperation was expected to strengthen the government's case against Scott Sullivan, the former CFO to whom Myers reported. Sullivan and other former WorldCom executives have been charged with securities fraud in connection with the company's accounting irregularities. In the aftermath of the bankruptcy, WorldCom's suppliers worried about getting paid for goods and services they had provided to the telecommunications firm. Although laid-off employees worried about receiving their full severance, a court order cleared the way for releasing $36 million in severance pay to thousands of former employees. The court also ruled that WorldCom could reduce the out-sized severance packages given to 19 senior managers. Service to WorldCom's millions of business and consumer customers has not yet been affected, but the company's future is unclear as the creditors' committee seeks to breathe new fiscal life into this bankrupt giant.[4]

"WorldCom Files for Bankruptcy; Largest U.S. Case," by Simon Romero and Riva D. Atlas

WorldCom, plagued by the rapid erosion of its profits and an accounting scandal that created billions in illusory earnings, last night submitted the largest bankruptcy filing in United States history.

The bankruptcy is expected to shake an already wobbling telecommunications industry, but is unlikely to have an immediate impact on customers, including the 20 million users of its MCI long-distance service.

The WorldCom filing listed more than $107 billion in assets, far surpassing those of Enron, which filed for bankruptcy last December. The WorldCom filing had been anticipated since the company disclosed in late June that it had improperly accounted for more than $3.8 billion of expenses.

Few experts or officials expect WorldCom's service to deteriorate noticeably, at least in the near term. "I want to assure the public that we do not believe this bankruptcy filing will lead to an immediate disruption of service to consumers," Michael K. Powell, chairman of the Federal Communications Commission, said last night.

But industry consultants said they could not imagine how the belt-tightening expected in bankruptcy would improve service that is already, in some respects, sloppy.

WorldCom's collapse has already reverberated through jittery financial markets, and is likely to be felt in the wider economy, with banks, suppliers and other telephone companies devising strategies to contain their exposure.

WorldCom, built through rapid acquisitions, accumulated $41 billion in debts. Founded in 1983 as LDDS Communications, it became the nation's second-largest long-distance company and the largest handler of Internet data.

Company executives said they intended to remain in business, and have been promised new financing from banks to do so. "We are going to aggressively go forward and restructure our operations," John W. Sidgmore, WorldCom's chief executive, said in an interview last night. "I think ultimately we will emerge as a stronger company."

While WorldCom has already cut its work force significantly, Mr. Sidgmore said last night that he did not expect further layoffs for the time being. He said he would remain WorldCom's chief but would be joined by a chief restructuring officer brought in by creditors.

Some creditors, however, have questioned whether Mr. Sidgmore, who has served on WorldCom's board for years, should remain in charge. Mr. Sidgmore took over as chief executive in late April after the board ousted Bernard J. Ebbers, one of the company's founders.

Shareholders, who owned what was once one of the world's most valuable companies, worth more than $100 billion at its peak, are expected to be virtually wiped out. With the bankruptcy filing, control passes instead to the banks and bondholders who financed WorldCom's growth.

Besides its own overambitious strategies and flawed accounting, WorldCom also fell victim to a glut of telecommunications capacity.

Cheap and plentiful financing allowed companies rapidly to build transcontinental and transoceanic fiber optic networks in the 1990's. The additional capacity resulted in lower prices for WorldCom's services, which include basic phone service and the transmission of Internet data for large companies.

Mr. Sidgmore said last night that he was opposed to breaking up WorldCom and selling its pieces, aside from an effort already under way to part with peripheral units like businesses in Latin America and some other operations. This approach would rule out selling UUNet, a large Internet backbone operation, or MCI.

But once the company reorganizes, and investors gain a better understanding of its twisted finances, WorldCom could become an attractive acquisition target, analysts say.

WorldCom's crisis deepened last month when it disclosed that Scott D. Sullivan, the chief financial officer, had devised a strategy that improperly accounted for $3.85 billion of expenses. Mr. Sullivan was fired by the board and David F. Myers, the financial controller, resigned.

The Securities and Exchange Commission has charged WorldCom with fraud and the Justice Department has begun a criminal investigation of its business practices.

In an attempt to regain its credibility, WorldCom's board elected two new members to replace Mr. Sullivan and Mr. Ebbers: Nicholas deB. Katzenbach, a private attorney who was attorney general in the Johnson administration; and Dennis R. Beresford, a former head of the Financial Accounting Standards Board and a professor of accounting at the Terry College of Business at the University of Georgia.

The two were also appointed to a special committee to oversee the internal investigation being led by William R. McLucas, the former chief of the enforcement division of the S.E.C.

WorldCom filed for bankruptcy shortly before 9 last night in Federal District Court in Manhattan.

Its international operations, which include companies in Brazil and Mexico, were not included.

The filing will relieve WorldCom of about $2 billion of interest payments in the coming year. Lower debt costs could allow WorldCom to compete on a stronger footing with its rivals, involving a potential price-cutting strategy that has analysts concerned about the wider strength of the telecommunications industry.

"WorldCom probably won't get any new big contracts from its current customers, but it probably won't lose any either, because of the difficulty and complexity involved in switching carriers," said Glen Macdonald, a vice president with Adventis, a consulting firm in Boston.

WorldCom, based in Clinton, Miss., scrambled in recent days to secure new financing from its banks after its cash dwindled to less than $300 million from more than $2 billion in May. WorldCom said last night that it had received commitments for up to $2 billion in additional bank financing. Such new loans to companies in bankruptcy receive top priority in repayment.

WorldCom must now deal with holders of $28 billion in bonds as well as 27 banks that loaned the company $2.65 billion last May.

But in contrast with other companies that have recently filed for bankruptcy, including Enron, WorldCom has many more tangible assets, generating actual revenues, lawyers said -- improving the odds that the company could emerge from bankruptcy as a going concern.

The creditors first in line to be repaid will be the three institutions -- Citigroup, J.P. Morgan and General Electric Capital -- that have pledged to arrange a loan of up to $2 billion, known as debtor in possession financing, to WorldCom. The lenders were comfortable pledging the funds in part because of the company's stream of customer payments, such as phone bills, one executive close to the company said last week. Citigroup is leading the new financing in part to protect what it is already owed by WorldCom.

WorldCom's bankruptcy filing, like Enron's last December, came on a Sunday. Companies often prefer to file over the weekend, because the status of any business transactions in process at the time of a filing would be open to question in court.

WorldCom's lenders and its bondholders were taking steps, even before the bankruptcy filing, to protect their claims. Just over a week ago, the banks that participated in the earlier $2.65 billion loan tried, unsuccessfully, to get a court order limiting WorldCom's access to the loan. The banks ultimately reached a settlement with WorldCom that placed few restrictions on the company's ability to use the cash.

"WorldCom Files for Bankruptcy" by Simon Romero, Riva D. Atlas, The New York Times, July 22, 2002   Copyright © 2002 by the New York Times Co.   Reprinted by permission.

"WorldCom Accounting Debacle Shows How Easy Fraud Can Be," by Jesse Drucker and Henny Sender

WorldCom Inc.'s disclosure of roughly $3.8 billion in improper accounting underscores how potential fraud on a huge scale can still be executed in a simple way.

WorldCom confessed to one of the oldest tricks in the book: not booking expenses immediately but pushing them into the future. Specifically, rather than recording what it paid other phone companies to help carry its customers' calls right away, it treated the costs as capital investments, which could be depreciated in pieces over time. The strategy gives an immediate boost to the net income by reducing expenses.

This was straightforward -- unlike the much-maligned "black box" accounting of Enron Corp., with its myriad off-balance-sheet partnerships and related-party transactions. And while the Enron debacle convinced investors to stay away from companies they couldn't easily understand, WorldCom's shocker may lead investors and analysts to back away from reliance on pro-forma profit indicators, such as earnings before interest, taxes, depreciation and amortization.

WorldCom is the latest in a growing list of companies, including Enron, Xerox Corp. and Reliant Resources Inc., to restate results to undo accounting moves that brightened financial reports. WorldCom's previous accounting obscured the fact that its basic business wasn't generating the healthy profits that investors were expecting. By counting expenses as capital investments, WorldCom was able to show a plumper bottom line to better suit Wall Street's expectations.

"It is a very simple accounting issue," says Stephen Ryan, an accounting professor at New York University's Leonard N. Stern School of Business. Prof. Ryan notes that companies frequently have to decide if something should be recorded as an expense today, in which case it is an operating expense, or tomorrow, in which case it is a capital investment.

"Think of the windows on your house," he says. "If you are doing something to maintain them, then you should expense them today. But if you are improving them, then you have created an asset, which you get to depreciate over time."

According to a WorldCom statement Tuesday, the Clinton, Miss., company transferred more than $3.8 billion in "line cost" expenses to its capital accounts over the past five quarters. WorldCom hasn't provided more detail about what those costs included, or what portions of its line costs were improperly capitalized. Line costs, according to the company's most recent annual report filed with the Securities and Exchange Commission, consist principally of access charges and transport charges -- broadly speaking, the fees WorldCom paid to other carriers for using their networks.

The "line costs" that WorldCom did report as an operating expense in 2001 totaled $14.74 billion in 2001, according to the company's income statement.

"Ongoing operating expenses of that type are things that you can't capitalize," says Doug Carmichael, director of the Center for Integrity in Financial Reporting at Baruch College in New York. "It's quite clear."

Telecommunications analysts agree that access charges like those paid by WorldCom, in general, would be considered operating expenses. "In our view, the typical access bill that a long-distance company would receive from a [regional Bell operating company] on a monthly basis would be expensed, not capitalized," says Daniel Zito, a telecom analyst at Legg Mason.

Some telecommunications analysts and accountants speculated Wednesday that the capitalized spending may also have included certain other costs, including salaries, interest on debt and perhaps even marketing or legal expenses. "It appears that certain line costs, perhaps labor costs for maintenance workers, for example, were booked as capital spending and amortized over a number of years instead of being expensed immediately as required" by generally accepted accounting principles, Simon Flannery, a telecommunications analyst at Morgan Stanley, wrote in a report.

The pending restatement raises further questions about beleaguered Arthur Andersen LLP, the auditor of Enron that was convicted of obstructing justice. While Arthur Andersen, WorldCom's auditor at the time, said it wasn't consulted or notified about the "line cost" capitalization, "auditors are supposed to look at material expenditures and make sure they are reported properly, this is accounting 101," says Izhak Sharav, an accounting professor at Columbia Business School in New York. Lawrence D. Morriss, a forensic accountant with Crossroads LLC, a consultancy, adds: "The growth of the balance sheet should have tipped off Arthur Andersen."

WorldCom's moves had the effect of enhancing the company's net income, but they had an even greater impact on its earnings before interest, taxes, depreciation and amortization -- the number that Wall Street prefers over net income for the telecommunications sector as well as other capital-intensive industries, such as cable television, media and wireless telecommunications.

WorldCom's disclosures could prompt some analysts to de-emphasize Ebitda, which already was under fire because it excludes so many normal business costs. "This is going to totally discredit Ebitda as a valuation method, and as a way to analyze the health of a company," says Thomas Lee, a wireless-telecommunications analyst at J.P. Morgan, who believes that net income or free cash flow may gain favor as performance indicators in its place. "That applies to cable, media, wireless. It's going to affect a lot of industries."

The accounting restatement that may come closest to WorldCom's in size came from Waste Management Inc. In 1998, it reduced its net income going back to 1991 with $3.54 billion in pretax charges and restatements. Among the items it reversed: capitalization of landfill costs. "Companies which have capital-intensive businesses and where fixed assets are a big part of the balance sheet offer the biggest opportunities for improper capitalizing of expenses," says Mr. Carmichael.

"WorldCom Accounting Debacle Shows How Easy Fraud Can Be." Wall Street Journal June 27, 2002 by Jesse Drucker and Henny Sender.

Questions For Discussion, Analysis, and Further Research

1. *For discussion and analysis:* The Sarbanes-Oxley Act requires the CEO of a publicly-held company to certify that the firm's financial statements are accurate (or risk being jailed and fined). Based on the information in Chapters 1 and 2 and the articles included in this chapter, what do you think a CEO might do to determine the accuracy of the firm's financial reports?

2. As your instructor directs, respond to this question individually, as part of a student team, or through participation in a classroom discussion.

3. *For discussion and analysis:* Which stakeholder groups are most affected when a company inflates its revenues or earnings so they look much higher than in reality? Which stakeholder groups are most affected when a company is exposed for fraudulently inflating its revenues or earnings? Explain your answer.

4. *For debate:* Should U.S. companies be allowed to make multimillion loans to executives, regardless of whether the managers use the money to invest in company stock or for some other purpose? Support your position using information from Chapters 1 and 2 as well as the articles in this chapter, supplemented with outside research if needed.

5. *For further research:* Use Internet or library sources to find out the status of regulatory and legal actions against WorldCom executives who have been implicated in the company's accounting scandal. What can other companies learn about detecting and preventing accounting fraud from the statements made by regulators, prosecutors, investigators, and the executives themselves? Summarize at least three ideas in a brief written or oral report to your class.

REFERENCES

1. Daniel Kadlec, "WorldCon: Nailed for the Biggest Bookkeeping Deception in History, a Fallen Telecom Giant Gives Investors One More Reason to Doubt Corporate Integrity," *Time,* July 8, 2002, pp. 20+; "Falling Star: How WorldCom Went from Highflier to Burnout," *Wall Street Journal*, August 2, 2002, www.wsj.com; Simon Romero and Riva D. Atlas, "WorldCom Files for Bankruptcy; Largest U.S. Case," *New York Times,* July 22, 2002, pp. A1+; "WorldCom to Cut Work Force in Europe, Middle East, Africa," *Wall Street Journal*, September 17, 2002, www.wsj.com.

2. Deborah Solomon, "WorldCom's Ex-Controller Pleads Guilty to Three Counts," *Wall Street Journal*, September 27, 2002, www.wsj.com.

3. Kadlec, "WorldCon;" Jesse Drucker and Henny Sender, "WorldCom Accounting Debacle Shows How Easy Fraud Can Be," *Wall Street Journal*, June 27, 2002, www.wsj.com; Susan Pulliam and Jared Sandberg, "New WorldCom Report to SEC Will Acknowledge More Flaws," *Wall Street Journal*, September 19, 2002, www.wsj.com; Jared Sandberg and Susan Pulliam, "WorldCom Finds More Errors; Restatement Will Be $7.2 Billion," *Wall Street Journal*, August 9, 2002, www.wsj.com; Floyd Norris, "Lies My C.F.O. Told Me, Act XIII," *New York Times,* June 30, 2002, pp. 5+.

4. Charles Haddad, "How Ebbers Kept the Board in His Pocket," *Business Week,* October 14, 2002, pp. 138-139; Solomon, "WorldCom's Ex-Controller Pleads Guilty to Three Counts;"

Shawn Young and Jared Sandberg, "WorldCom Can Pay Severance in Full to Its Laid-Off

Workers," *Wall Street Journal*, October 2, 2002, www.wsj.com.

NAME INDEX

Creswell, Julie, 28n32
Criner, Oscar, 93–94
Crumbley, D. Larry, 75n45
Cullinan, Charles, 53

D
Delainey, David W., 86
Deutsch, Claudia H., 76n52
Donaldson, Thomas, 27n21, 78n65, 79n68
Drucker, Jesse, 103–104, 106n3
Drucker, Peter, 34
Dubinsky, Joan Elise, 71n20
Duncan, David B., 93–94
Duncan, John, 84
Dwyer, Paula, 69n3, 71n16
Dyson, Esther, 44–45

E
Ebbers, Bernard J., 99, 102
Ebert, Ronald J., 26n17
Eichenwald, Kurt, 24n2, 27n23, 71n18–19, 77n55, 92–96, 97n3–4
Entwistle, Andrew, 86
Enzi, Michael B., 39
Eyres, Bill, 28n27–28

F
Fastow, Andrew, 36–38, 82
Feder, Barnaby J., 24n4
Felo, Andrew J., 73n29, 79n73
Fineman, Howard, 69n3, 69n4, 69n5
Flannery, Simon, 104
France, Mike, 30n43
Frederick, Adrienne Carter, 76n50
Frederick, Jim, 75n44
Freeman, R. Edward, 26n19, 27n20

G
Gasparino, Charles, 71n17
Gilbert, Jackie, 26n14
Gimein, Mark, 71n17
Glater, Jonathan D., 26n15, 69n4, 72n21–22, 77n59
Golden, Neil, 76n49
Goldstein, Sidney, 25n12
Gordon, Kathryn, 78n66
Greenberg, Herb, 24n4, 69n3
Greenspan, Alan, 34

Mack, Toni, 88n1
Malone, Farrell, 95
Markton, Jerry, 69n3, 73n30
Mason, Julie, 72n26
Mason, Tania, 27n22
McGinn, Daniel, 24n2
McLean, Bethany, 88n1
McLucas, William R., 102
McNamee, Mike, 75n42, 77n55
Mehta, Stephanie N., 30n44
Mescon, Michael H., 25n9
Meyer, Michael J., 26n17
Millman, Gregory J., 78n65, 79n71, 80n79
Miyake, Maiko, 78n66
Morgenson, Gretchen, 28n31, 71n17, 74n36
Morriss, Lawrence D., 104
Myers, David F., 33, 95, 99–100, 102

N
Norris, Floyd, 106n3
Nusbaum, Marci Alboher, 78n64, 80n75, 80n77, 80n78

O
O'Meara, Kelly Patricia, 83–85, 89n2
Olofson, Roy, 63
Opdyke, Jeff D., 29n35–37
Oppel, Richard A., 24n5
Orenstein, Susan, 80n78

P
Pacelle, Mitchell, 89n3
Paine, Lynn Sharp, 60
Paltrow, Scot J., 77n54
Parloff, Roger, 27n22
Phillips, Trevor, 28n27–28
Pitt, Harvey L., 95
Pollack, Andrew, 72n25
Powell, Michael K., 101
Pulliam, Susan, 24n4, 75n46, 106n3

R
Rathvon, Richard, 86
Reason, Tim, 76n52
Reingold, Jennifer, 74n40
Richardson, John E., 26n17
Rigas, John, 43, 85

Ringer, Richard C., 28n29
Robinson-Jacobs, Karen, 98n6
Roman, Monica, 70n11
Romero, Simon, 101–103, 105
Ross, Andrew, 75n47
Rossant, John, 72n27
Ryan, Stephen, 103

S
Sandberg, Jared, 24n4, 69n3, 75n46, 106n3, 106n4
Sapsford, Jathon, 28n33, 74n37
Schiesel, Seth, 24n4
Schroeder, Michael, 26n16
Schultz, Ellen E., 29n39
Scott, A., 75n43
Seglin, Jeffrey L., 78n61, 79n69
Sender, Henny, 103–104, 106n3
Serwer, Andy, 75n43
Shanks, Thomas, 26n17
Shapiro, Andy, 47
Sharav, Izhak, 104
Sheeley, Glenn, 30n45
Sidgmore, John W., 101–102
Siegel, Michael A., 86
Sierra, Brian, 85
Simpson, Liz, 29n42
Sinclair, Upton, 1
Skilling, Jeffrey K., 86
Sloan, Allan, 29n36
Smith, N. Craig, 25n12
Smith, Stephanie D., 75n44, 76n50
Solomon, Deborah, 106n2, 106n4
Sommer, Jeff, 74n38
Stead, Bette Ann, 26n14
Stellin, Susan, 73n32
Stern, Linda, 79n68
Stires, David, 29n36
Stoffer, Harry, 27n24
Strauss, Gary, 69n5
Strong, Kelly C., 28n29
Sullivan, Scott D., 33, 95, 100, 102
Sutton, Steve, 53
Swartz, Jon, 27n5
Sylla, Richard, 35

T
Taylor, Steven A., 28n29
Tedlow, Richard, 58
Temple, Nancy, 93–95
Thill, John V., 25n9
Thornton, Emily, 73n34
Tilney, Schuyler, 37

V
Valesquez, Manuel, 26n17
Venkataraman, Sankaran, 26n19, 27n20
Verschoor, Curtis C., 79n70
Vrana, Debora, 72n24

W
Waddock, Sandra, 27n20
Waksal, Samuel, 41
Warner, Steve, 13
Watkins, Sherron, 62
Wee, Heesun, 70n6
Weil, Jonathan, 71n15
Weissmann, Andrew, 93
White, Thomas I., 25n10
Wilke, John R., 89n3
Williams, Dean, 27n22
Winokur, Herbert "Pug," 84
Wyatt, Mary, 86

Y
Young, Shawn, 106n4
Yung, Katherine, 80n75

Z
Zisman, Stuart, 62
Zito, Daniel, 104

SUBJECT INDEX